THE COST AND FINANCING OF SOCIAL SECURITY

THE BROOKINGS INSTITUTION

The Brookings Institution—Devoted to Public Service through Research and Training in the Social Sciences—was incorporated on December 8, 1927. Broadly stated, the Institution has two primary purposes: the first is to aid constructively in the development of sound national policies; and the second is to offer training of a supergraduate character to students of the social sciences.

The responsibility for the final determination of the Institution's policies and its program of work for the administration of its endowment is vested in a self-perpetuating board of trustees. It is the function of the trustees to make possible the conduct of scientific research under the most favorable conditions, and to safeguard the independence of the research staff in the pursuit of their studies and in the publication of the results of such studies. It is not a part of their function to determine, control, or influence the conduct of particular investigations or the conclusions reached, but only to approve the principal fields of investigation to which the available funds are to be allocated, and to satisfy themselves with reference to the intellectual competence and scientific integrity of the staff. Major responsibility for "formulating general policies and coordinating the activities of the Institution" is vested in the president. The by-laws provide also that "there shall be an advisory council selected by the president from among the scientific staff of the Institution."

Authors of studies published by the Institution have had the advice, criticism, and assistance both of an administrative officer and of a cooperating committee selected from the staff. In manuscript accepted for publication, the author has freedom to present his final interpretations and conclusions, although they may not necessarily be concurred in by some or all of those who cooperate with him or by other members of the staff. The Institution in publishing the work assumes the responsibility that it meets reasonable tests of scholarship and presents data and conclusions worthy of public consideration.

BOARD OF TRUSTEES

The Cost and Financing

of

Social Security

By

LEWIS MERIAM

and

KARL SCHLOTTERBECK

With a Chapter on Veterans' Benefits

By

MILDRED MARONEY

ERRATUM

Page 102, line 21, "21 billion dollars" should read "2 billion dollars."

Washington, D. C.

THE BROOKINGS INSTITUTION

1950

Printed in the United States of America
The McArdle Printing Co.
Washington, D. C.

PREFACE

The Congress now has under consideration proposals for social security programs which are elaborate and costly. Most important among them are the recommendations for compulsory health insurance and for amending the old-age and survivors insurance system to make it an almost universal retirement system with high benefits.

The old-age and survivors insurance system in its present form involves constantly mounting costs over a fifty-year period. Great confusion has been engendered in the public mind because of the assumption that these costs can be gradually provided for through the application of ordinary insurance principles. That is, it is widely believed that the social security taxes now being paid furnish the resources from which the future benefits will be paid. The fact is that a practically universal governmental system cannot successfully apply the actuarial legal reserve devices of private voluntary insurance systems. As the present system operates, no real reserve funds with which to meet future requirements are accumulated. The benefits will have to be paid out of future taxes.

The future demands upon the government for benefit payments—to be paid out of future taxes—will be so great that it appears to us essential that they be given full consideration now before the commitments are made. The demands for cash for benefits must be studied in the light of other governmental cash requirements for national defense, foreign relations, veterans' benefits, interest on the public debt, and all other activities of government.

This book focuses attention on these issues and examines the financial difficulties which may arise if present Congresses attempt to commit future generations to the extent proposed.

The criticisms that the authors direct against the unnecessarily costly and, from the standpoint of public

v

finance, futile use of some of the concepts of private voluntary insurance should not be construed as opposition to adequate provision from the public treasury for persons who are in need. In the concluding chapter the writers present in outline four broad types of social security systems that may be considered, ranging in cost from one that supplies for all in need a reasonable level of living upward to the elaborate, almost universal retirement system recommended by the Administration. They recommend a true pay-as-you-go system under which persons now in need will have those needs met from current revenues. They would have the present generation provide for those who are incapable of self-support in a manner that the current economy can support, and they would trust future generations to take similar action in the light of the economic conditions of their day.

The authors of this study, Lewis Meriam and Karl Schlotterbeck, have had the advice of a co-operating committee consisting of Cleona Lewis, Harold W. Metz, and myself. Mildred Maroney contributed the chapter on veterans' benefits but did not participate in the writing of the other chapters.

The authors wish to have recorded their obligations to A. Evelyn Breck, the editor for the Institution, and Medora M. Richardson, assistant to Mr. Meriam.

H. G. Moulton,
President

The Brookings Institution
January 1950

vi

CONTENTS

PART III. ANALYSIS OF THE OVER-ALL
SECURITY PROGRAM

The study upon which this publication is based was made possible by funds granted by THE MAURICE AND LAURA FALK FOUNDATION of Pittsburgh. However, the FALK FOUNDATION is not the author, publisher, or proprietor of this publication and is not to be understood as approving or disapproving by virtue of its grant any of the statements and views expressed herein.

INTRODUCTION

The national administration has proposed and the Congress has under consideration recommendations for social security programs more elaborate and costly than any other nation has yet adopted.

Ensuing chapters will present and analyze these proposals insofar as they affect cost. Here it need only be said that the most sweeping of the proposals call for (1) the introduction of a national system of compulsory health insurance and (2) the radical revision of the present old-age and survivors insurance system through (a) introducing disability benefits, (b) increasing the amount of earnings subject to tax, (c) revising the benefit formula in ways that will substantially increase benefits and costs, and (d) greatly expanding the coverage.

The electorate in a democracy can intelligently consider government proposals for new and extended activities only when the costs of such proposals are readily apparent, because they call for financing in current or early budgets. They can weigh the advantages to be obtained against costs in terms of taxes to be paid immediately or in the near future. Unfortunately, the present program is so designed that the vast magnitude of prospective future costs is understood only by persons who have given close study to the subject.

· The present book has been prepared in the belief that, before social security systems are adopted which for many years to come will have constantly expanding and ultimately stupendous costs, the facts as to these costs, insofar as they can be forecast, should be presented and analyzed. In some cases, notably in unemployment compensation, no dependable forecasts are possible, because in that program costs are largely dependent on economic conditions. For that program attention has to be directed not to the costs themselves but to the factors which will determine costs.

1

As the costs and cost factors presented in the ensuing chapters will show, the sums required will reach such proportions that they may have a profound effect on the entire economy. Insufficient public attention has been given to these economic possibilities. The explanation is twofold. First, as already noted, the immediate cash requirements of some of the programs are small and afford no indication of ultimate costs. Second, the tendency has been for the government and the people to consider each program as something separate and apart. To gauge the possible impact on the economy as a whole, the future costs of all the programs must be combined. The aggregate future costs indicate the magnitude of the problem of financing.

Some students, government officials, and legislators apparently assume that future costs, even of great magnitude, should occasion no concern. The productive capacity of the United States, they hold, has increased so steadily in the past that a like increase can safely be anticipated for the future. Thus, when the children and the grandchildren are called upon to produce the cash required for the benefits now promised, they will be able to do so without difficulty.

Such a confident attitude hardly seems warranted in view of the highly unstable world in which we live. It is entirely possible that changes will take place, externally or even internally, that will retard or even prevent the hoped for and anticipated upward progress in productive efficiency. As postwar experience is demonstrating, conditions over which the nation does not have complete control may dictate heavy expenditures for national defense and for aid to foreign governments. Both man power and other resources may have to be diverted to activities that are essential for national security, although they place heavy burdens on the individual.

Moreover, future generations, like our own, will encounter competition among the various activities of government for available public funds. One of the great issues that government confronts is that of priorities. Today, for example, the funds spent for national defense and international aid could be effectively used for domestic activities, but the predominant view is that protection of the nation against possible aggressors has a clear priority. There is nothing to justify a belief that future generations will not confront similar issues in allocating production. Freedom in meeting their problems may be complicated by inherited commitments for social security and interest on the public debt. They may prefer larger expenditures for education, housing, or highways.

Finally, social security systems which promise only fixed money benefits in the distant future may fail to provide the real security expected because of a progressively rising level of prices. Two facts are obvious: (1) real social security depends upon the goods and services that money benefits will buy at the time the benefits are paid, and (2) people can, in the main, consume only goods and services currently produced. Hence if through governmental action or other causes an upward spiraling of prices takes place, the utility of the social security system is impaired or even destroyed.

It is sometimes maintained that the dangers of an upward spiraling of prices can be safely ignored in framing a social security system because, if it takes place, the government can raise the amount of the benefits. Current proposals for revision of old-age and survivors insurance, for instance, include increases in money benefits for those already receiving them to offset price increases since 1939. The amounts involved are relatively small. It must be remembered, however, that the number of beneficiaries will increase every year for the next fifty years. Increasing benefits for all on the retired list will become more and more burdensome as time goes on. Factors such as these preclude accepting the assumption that future increases in production will solve all problems of cost and financing.

Costs and the major factors influencing costs are presented and analyzed in the first part of the book for the four principal programs: (1) old-age, survivors, and disability insurance, (2) unemployment compensation, (3) health insurance, and (4) public assistance. Part II deals with certain tangential problems that are significant elements in considering cost and financing: (1) the very poor, who probably will not be provided for by social insurance systems of the present American pattern; (2) veterans' benefits, which are significant because of the magnitude of the expenditures and because they may overlap and duplicate social security benefits; and (3) private pension and retirement systems, which are significant because of their interrelationships with any social security system.

The final part of the book starts with a summary of costs and benefits, based in the main on the first four chapters. The next chapter deals with the question of how the costs can be financed and analyzes the nature, purpose, and use of reserves. This is followed by a chapter on the budgetary impact of the social security systems. The final chapter presents conclusions.

PART I

MAJOR SOCIAL SECURITY PROGRAMS

The objective in Part I is to consider the costs and the factors which will determine costs with respect to four major social security programs: old-age, survivors, and disability insurance, unemployment compensation, compulsory health insurance, and public assistance. In these four fields existing arrangements and proposed additions and changes will be discussed.

No attempt has been made to treat systems covering special classes of employees, such as the railroad workers, numerous classes of government employees—federal, state, and local—and employees of private organizations. Such systems, insofar as they are retained, will add to the over-all costs of formal systems for providing social security.

Existing state systems for temporary disability are omitted, because they presumably will be modified in the event of the adoption of general systems covering temporary and permanent disability. Workmen's Compensation is omitted as it is not involved in current proposals for change.

CHAPTER I
OLD-AGE, SURVIVORS, AND
DISABILITY INSURANCE

Over the years private insurance, operated according to specific government regulations, has won the confidence of the American people. Individuals and families have increasingly turned to insurance for their minimum requirements for social and economic protection. This confidence in private insurance has been based on its soundness, which in turn has rested on the establishment and maintenance of financial reserves. Adoption of the term "insurance" by the proponents of social security was a stroke of promotional genius. Thus social security has capitalized on the good will of private insurance and, through the establishment of a reserve fund, has clothed itself with an aura of financial soundness. In fact, however, the soundness of old-age and survivors insurance rests not on the Social Security Reserve Fund but on the federal power to tax and to borrow. Public confusion on this point perhaps accounts in large measure for the attention given to the welfare aspects of social security and the lack of consideration for future costs and who must inevitably pay them.

Both proponents and critics of the existing system have been in agreement for several years that radical changes are required.[1] Those who favor this system—including its underlying concepts and philosophy—seek broad extensions of such vital matters as (1) coverage, (2) the earnings subject to the tax, (3) the benefit formula, (4) new and additional benefits, (5) the qualifying conditions, (6)

---

[1] ". . . there is need for a review of the old-age and survivors insurance program, covering not only the benefit formula, the coverage of the system, and the scope of protection afforded, but also contributions and financial policy. . . ." *Federal Old-Age and Survivors Insurance Trust Fund,* S. Doc. 160, 80 Cong. 2 sess., p. 32.

8

special provisions for women, and (7) earnings after retirement.

Early in the Eighty-first Congress a bill was introduced in the House—H.R.2893—which embodied the recommendations of the Administration with respect to changes. This bill was supported by numerous groups who believe not only in "cradle-to-the-grave" social insurance but in levels of benefits substantially higher than are necessary merely to protect against want. The concepts of relating benefits to earnings in the best years and of covering all earnings not in excess of $4,800 a year were introduced. The general welfare was to be promoted by including a high measure of the pooling of risks involved in insurance, with the inescapable concomitant of reducing the freedom of the individual in determining how his earnings are to be expended. Risk bearing by the individual was to be curtailed. Costs of all benefits were to be spread in the manner prescribed in the bill.

The Ways and Means Committee held comprehensive hearings on H.R. 2893. Leading officers of the Social Security Administration and the Bureau of Internal Revenue explained the extremely complicated provisions of the bill. Official estimates of costs were presented. Witnesses were heard for and against the various proposals, some appearing as individuals, others as representatives of organizations which had particular interests. Among the witnesses were some concerned primarily with social policy; others with narrow issues of immediate consequence to themselves; and still others whose training and experience were such that they could give expert testimony on the complicated technical matters that are so difficult for the uninitiated to understand.

On August 15, 1949 the chairman of the Ways and Means Committee introduced a bill—H.R. 6000—which was followed by a majority and a minority report. This bill passed the House on October 5, 1949 under a rule that did not permit the offering of amendments from the floor or by the minority members of the Ways and Means Committee. The position taken, not without substantial merit, was that H.R. 6000 was too intricate and technical for piecemeal amendment by persons not conversant with all its complexities.

The bill that passed the House calls for extensive liberalizing changes in the present OASI system. When contrasted with the Administration proposals as embodied in H.R. 2893, on the other hand, it could be characterized as comparatively modest. It is a compromise.

Passage of H.R. 6000 presented the question whether the main text of our study should deal with the radical proposals of H.R. 2893 or the compromise provisions of H.R. 6000. It was decided that the main text should deal with H.R. 2893, for two reasons: first, because it shows the full measure of the conception of the Administration as to what is essential to the public welfare; and, second, because the scope and provisions of the final bill which may emerge from House and Senate deliberations are as yet unknown. Omission of H.R. 6000 from discussion in the main text does not mean that its provisions with respect to controversial issues will be ignored. They will be briefly summarized in footnotes. By this method it is hoped the confusion can be avoided which would result from attempting to consider two different and complicated systems simultaneously.

PROPOSED CHANGES

Before figures for the cost of the plan embodied in H.R. 2893 are introduced, the major changes it would make in the existing system and the reasons for them will be summarized.

Coverage. The existing law for administrative and other reasons excludes from coverage several numerically important classes.[2] These include: (1) agricultural laborers, (2) domestic servants in private homes, (3) casual workers, (4) persons who are self-employed or working on their own account, (5) employees of private nonprofit, religious, charitable, scientific, or educational agencies, (6) employees of state governments or their instrumentalities, (7) employees of the federal government, (8) employees of the railroads covered under the Railroad Retirement Act.

The exclusion of such classes involves a substantial discrimination against them. Since the cost of all benefits now being paid, and of those which will be paid in the next few years, will greatly exceed the taxes paid by the beneficiaries and by employers on their account, those included under the system are thus given the privilege of drawing benefits paid for by others. Under OASI these so-called "windfall benefits" are paid regardless of whether the recipient is or is not in need. It is extremely difficult in a democracy to justify windfall benefits for persons with comfortable means on the ground that it was practicable to cover them, while denying comparable benefits to some of the most needy classes in the country on the ground that it was administratively inexpedient to include them.

If an employee covered under the present system shifts to an uncovered occupation before he has attained a fully insured status, he loses all or a part of the protection he would have acquired had he remained in covered employment. His payments and those of his employer on his account are in many cases forfeited to the fund, although if he had been under the system long enough he might have had some temporary extended insurance for his eligible survivors.[3]

[2] For the complete list and the precise wording, see the Social Security Act, as amended in 1939, Title II, sec. 209 (b), 53 Stat. 1373.

[3] Louis O. Shudde and George E. Immerwahr, *Old-Age and Survivors Insurance Analysis of Long-Range Cost Factors*, Social Security Administration, Actuarial Study 21 (September 1946), pp. 13-18, contains a technical discussion of insured status.

The distinction between covered employed and uncovered self-employed has proved to be vague. The law did not provide that payment by the employee or the employer of the pay-roll tax should be the criterion of eligibility. Eligibility turned on employment in a covered position, whether or not the taxes had been paid.

Controversies arose as to whether certain classes of workers were operating on their own account as independent businessmen and were hence excluded under the terms of the existing act, or whether they were in substance employees of the concern upon which they were economically dependent for their current business. They were not employees of the concern according to the common law concept of the employer-employee relationship, but neither were they as economically independent of the concern as is a businessman who buys from producers and distributors in his discretion or contracts to render service for different parties as he sees fit. Experience has demonstrated two points: (1) that there is a wide twilight zone between the employer-employee relationship of the common law and the clear-cut definite status of working on one's own account; and (2) that within this twilight zone there are numerous combinations—both quantitative and qualitative—of the several factors which might be regarded as indicating economic dependence or independence. This complicated and controversial subject has consumed a substantial and costly amount of time of the Federal Security Agency, the Bureau of Internal Revenue, the Congress and its committees, the courts, the companies affected, and the workers involved and their associations.[4]

---

[4] For examples, see testimony of Harold Packer, Assistant General Counsel, Federal Security Agency, p. 2206; statement of Wallace E. Campbell, Vice President of the Fuller Brush Co., p. 2415; statement of Leonard J. Calhoun, attorney for 24 companies of direct distributors, p. 2448; statement of Mrs. Olga S. Ross, Executive Secretary, National Council of Salesmen's Organizations, Inc., p. 2393 in *Social Security Act Amendments of 1949*, Hearings before the House Committee on Ways and Means on H.R. 2893, 81 Cong. 1 sess., Pt. 2. Hereafter cited as Ways and Means Committee Hearings, 1949.

Experience has abundantly demonstrated that if this kind of a system is to be operated at all and is to be supported in part through general taxation, practically all workers should be covered—regardless of the nature of their work. To prevent losses and forfeitures on movement from one occupation to another, complete coverage is essential. H.R. 2893 goes a long way in this direction, although for practical as distinct from theoretical reasons it continues to exclude federal employees and railroad employees who have systems regarded by them as definitely more advantageous.[5] For constitutional reasons, coverage of the employees of state and local governments is optional with those governments,[6] but policemen and firemen may not be included.[7]

Earnings subject to tax. Under the present system taxes are collected and benefits paid with respect to the first $3,000 of annual earnings in covered employment. Since the adoption of the original act in 1935, the general level of money wages has greatly increased. Benefits based on the first $250 of monthly earnings, according to the existing formula, are no longer adequate to supply a living according to a reasonable minimum health and decency standard for persons who are entirely dependent on those benefits. Such persons may have to ask for supplementation through means test public assistance. H.R. 2893 proposes to base taxes and benefits on the first $400 of monthly earnings.

[5] See testimony of Lewis H. Fisher against inclusion of federal employees, the same, p. 1956.

[6] H.R. 2893, sec. 204.

[7] H.R. 6000 does not extend coverage to persons engaged in agriculture (whether as self-employed individuals or as employees), federal employees covered under retirement systems, members of the armed forces, railroad employees, the self-employed of designated professional groups, and certain other smaller groups. The committee gave consideration to the inclusion of agricultural employees, to self-employed farm operators, and to other self-employed groups excluded, but reached the conclusion that further study was required. *Social Security Act Amendments of 1949,* 81 Cong. 1 sess., H. Rept. 1300, p. 9.

This change would greatly increase both the revenue from the pay-roll taxes and the costs of the benefits.

The proposal to tax wages and salaries and the earnings of the self-employed up to $4,800 and to apply the benefit formula up to that amount has given rise to wide differences of opinion.

The arguments in favor of it may be summarized as follows:

1. Because of the upward spiral of wages, $4,800 is now about the equivalent of $3,000, the present upper limit.

2. Benefits under the existing law have been rendered inadequate by increased living costs. Provision of adequate benefits calls for liberalizing the formula, raising the maximum earnings to which it applies, and basing the benefits on the average for the best five consecutive years instead of on the average during coverage.

3. The American system is designed to insure against loss of earnings through old age or other covered contingencies. It is not designed simply to provide a minimum amount upon the happening of an included contingency.[8]

Opponents of the proposed increase to $4,800 do not agree that a social insurance system should be designed to replace a definite proportion of former earnings of the retired workers, but rather to assure them of a sufficient cash income to prevent want and enable them to live according to a reasonable minimum health and decency standard even if they are entirely dependent on their social security benefits. Social insurance, according to this point of view, should put a floor of protection under the insured workers. If persons with reasonably good earnings desire more than such a minimum, they should obtain it through their own voluntary efforts.

Believers in the floor of protection concept are not in agreement as to the amount of benefit and the method of

[8] See testimony of Arthur J. Altmeyer, Commissioner for the Social Security Administration, Ways and Means Committee Hearings, 1949, pp. 1164, 1205.

determining it.[9] Some favor the flat uniform benefit such
as is used in the British system where the idea is to supply
a reasonable minimum to all eligibles and leave them free
to use their income after taxes as they see fit.[10] The amount
of this benefit would be determined through budgetary
studies, and it would provide a specific amount for each
primary beneficiary with additional amounts for each eligible dependent.

Another group does not object to relating benefits and
taxes to earnings up to $3,000 as at present but is strongly
opposed to raising the earnings covered to $4,800.[11] This
group recognizes the fact that present benefits have to be
raised to offset the upward spiral of wages and prices, but
they make the point that necessary changes can be effected
by changing the existing formula without any increase in
the amount of earnings covered. Their arguments against
the change may be summarized as follows, although it
should be understood that they do not all necessarily advance the same arguments.

1. The cost of the system will be materially increased by paying
large benefits with respect to earnings above $3,000, yet this increase
in cost is unnecessary if the system is to be confined to its proper
purpose of insuring against need.

2. Higher taxes coupled with the larger base will increase the
inherent difficulties in the financial administration of the system,
particularly the surplus funds that accumulate in the early years.

3. Persons with earnings over $3,000 should be left free to use
the largest possible portion above that amount as they see fit.

9 See Ways and Means Committee Hearings, 1949, testimony of W. Rulon
Williamson, pp. 1484-1502; statement of Dorrance C. Bronson, pp. 1625-43;
and statement of Joseph A. Schafer, pp. 2375-85.

10 The British system requires a uniform contribution from all workers in
the same general class without any variation with respect to the amount of
their earnings. Thus, an unskilled worker and the top official in the company
for which he works make the same contributions and get the same primary
benefits. Whether one draws more from the fund than the other will depend
primarily on the number and type of his eligible dependents.

11 For example, see testimony of M. Albert Linton, President, Provident
Mutual Life Insurance Co. and member of the Advisory Council on Social
Security, Ways and Means Committee Hearings, 1949, especially pp. 1378-79.

The farmer or the independent businessman may be able to get far greater protection for himself and his dependents if he uses his savings in his own enterprise. Any worker through home ownership, voluntary insurance, or other forms of saving can adapt his program to his individual needs and those of his family.

4. Raising the amount of earnings covered will further complicate public and private retirement systems. As the taxes are raised to pay for increasing costs of benefits, many of these systems may have to be abolished entirely.

5. As the taxes increase, private saving which has supplied funds for capital investment may be diminished.[12] It is also feared that granting an increase of 1 per cent of the basic benefit for each year of covered service will tend to destroy in many persons the incentive to save, as the benefits will appear more nearly adequate to meet their requirements.

6. Basing benefits on the first $4,800 of earnings would increase the cost of the windfall benefits. When the system is mature of course, an upper bracket earner will be paying in taxes an amount approximately sufficient to pay for an annuity with a private insurance company yielding comparable benefits to those he would receive under the proposed system. However, those who retire in the earlier years will receive, in return for the contributions they will make through pay-roll taxes, benefits far in excess of those they could obtain through like payments with a private company. The benefits received in excess of those that could have been procured under a private annuity contract are referred to as windfall benefits. The higher the covered earnings, the more costly would be the windfall benefits.[13]

Proponents of the flat sum uniform budgetary benefits point out that such a system would result in a material saving over the present system in the costs of administration. It would no longer be necessary to operate the expensive system required to record and tabulate the earnings of all workers from entrance into the labor force

[12] The evidence indicates that the 1 per cent tax collected originally did not discourage the purchase of voluntary insurance. It is alleged that a desire to supplement the present small old-age and survivors benefits has encouraged rather than discouraged the purchase of ordinary life insurance. It does not follow, however, that raising the amount of earnings subject to tax, the amount of tax, and the size of the benefits will continue to have the same effect.

[13] For example, see *Old-Age and Survivors Insurance*, S. Doc. 149, 80 Cong. 2 sess., pp. 64-66.

until retirement on benefits or until death, if death comes before retirement,[14] nor would good public relations require the maintenance of a network of local offices now operated to answer the myriad of questions which are inherent in administering so complicated a system.[15]

The benefit formula. The existing system bases benefits on the average monthly wages during coverage. The first step in applying the formula is to add to 40 per cent of the first $50 of average monthly wages 10 per cent of the remainder, which cannot exceed $200. One per cent of the total thus obtained is added for each year of covered service. The resulting aggregate is the primary monthly benefit for the retired worker himself. All other benefits are fractions of this primary benefit. The minimum primary benefit is $10 a month and the maximum of all benefits combined must not in any case exceed $85.

The formula proposed in H.R. 2893 bases benefits on the average earnings in the best five consecutive years of coverage. The new formula for determining the primary benefit involves three factors: (1) the basic amount, (2) the continuation factor, and (3) the length of covered service. They may be described as follows: (1) "An individual's 'basic amount' means 50 per centum of the first $75 of his average monthly wage plus 15 per centum of the next $325 of such wage." (Sec. 202(b).) (2) The basic amount thus obtained is multiplied by the continuation factor. "An individual's 'continuation factor' means the quotient obtained by dividing the number of his years of coverage after his starting date by the number of his elapsed years." (Sec. 202 (2) (c).) Thus a man con-

---

[14] Dorrance C. Bronson testified: "I hope you will examine the required record-keeping system, sort of a Frankenstein of the machine age, an exhibitionism of ability to keep track of the minutiae appertaining to this so-called contributory system." Ways and Means Committee Hearings, 1949, p. 1625.

[15] H.R. 6000 raises the amount of earnings subject to the special taxes and employed in determining benefits from the present $3,000 a year to $3,600.

tinuously covered from his starting date to age 65 [16] would have a continuation factor of 100 per cent. (3) To the product of the basic amount multiplied by the continuation factor is added "1 per centum of his basic amount for each of his years of coverage." (Sec. 202 (a).)

These changes in the benefit formula would result in substantially higher benefits and costs. Thus should there be a gradually upward movement in the level of money wages, it will be almost fully reflected in the amount of benefits, for in many cases the best five consecutive years will be the five immediately preceding retirement. If the unexpected should happen, and the level of money wages fall, the amount of benefits would not be materially affected immediately, for then the best five consecutive years may be in earlier periods of service. Use of the best five consecutive years tends to increase the amount of benefits and to add to the cost of the system. Figures showing the costs involved in this plan are presented at page 27.[17]

Other benefits provided. The most radical change proposed in H.R. 2893 is the introduction of disability bene-

[16] For women the bill proposes to make 60 the age for eligibility for old-age benefits.

[17] H.R. 6000 rejects the proposal to base benefits on the best five consecutive years of service and retains the present practice of using the average wage, although with some modifications in the methods employed in determining the average. The basic amount used in the formula is 50 per cent of the first $100 of average monthly earnings, plus 10 per cent of the remainder, which cannot exceed $200. The length of service increment of one per cent of the base amount for each year of covered service used in the present law and recommended for continuance in H.R. 2893 is reduced to one half of one per cent. The minimum primary benefit under H.R. 6000 would be $25 as contrasted with $10 under the present law. The committee states: "Persons who retire after 1949 would have their benefits computed under the . . . new formula, with resulting benefits approximately double the average benefits payable today." H. Rept. 1300, 81 Cong. 1 sess., p. 6. Benefits for persons already retired would be increased on the average by about 70 per cent. "Increases would range from 50 percent for highest benefit groups to as much as 150 percent for lowest benefit groups." The same. The minority report would retain the present $3,000 limit, eliminate entirely the length of service increment, but base benefits on the average salary for the highest ten consecutive years. The same, p. 158. Neither the majority nor the minority has embraced the recommended philosophy of insuring part of purchasing power up to the high level of $4,800, as recommended in H.R. 2893.

fits. The three principal ones are for (1) total disability, (2) temporary disability, and (3) maternity. Provision is also made for disabled children over 18 years of age together with disabled husbands or widowers of women workers, who had attained an insured status prior to their retirement on account of age or disability or prior to their death either before or after retirement.

From a social and economic standpoint provision for disabled workers and their dependents seems far more justifiable than providing large benefits after very short service to people who are not in need. It must be remembered, however, that scarcely anything in the field of insurance is more difficult to administer than disability benefits.[18]

The dangers of abuse are great. Under the proposed plan the duty of preventing abuse would have to be entrusted to government employees controlled and directed by a politically appointed officer. At each election, national, state, and in the case of big cities municipal, he will be concerned with the success of his political party at the polls. If he himself tries to keep politics out of administration, he will have to withstand the demands of national, state, and local political workers who know the effectiveness of favors in influencing an election. He may be asked only to look the other way, at least until the elections are over.

Political and psychological factors would play a large part in determining the cost of disability insurance. No country that has installed such a system accurately predicted in advance anything approaching the actual costs. Government agencies which promote its adoption may be suspected of understating costs in their eagerness to get

[18] For statement of Judd C. Benson of the National Association of Life Underwriters, see Ways and Means Committee Hearings, 1949, p. 1425. See also statement of M. Albert Linton appearing for Life Insurance Association of America, the same, p. 1408.

laws on the books, but the difficulty is probably far deeper than over-optimism. The necessity of earning a living and supporting a family makes many a person hold a job despite partial disability, either temporary or permanent. Relieve them of the necessity, and thousands will take the position that having paid the taxes they are entitled to the benefits.[19]

Qualifying conditions. The existing law requires that a person to be eligible for an old-age benefit must have one calendar quarter of coverage for each two elapsed quarters after 1936 or age 21 and before age 65, but in no case are more than 40 quarters of coverage required. H.R. 2893 proposes to reduce the requirement to not less than one quarter of coverage for each four elapsing after 1936 or after the quarter in which he attained the age of 21, whichever is later, and in no case less than six quarters.[20] The reason for the change is that the old provi-

---

[19] H.R. 6000 provides under the insurance system only for permanent and total disability. Its report reads: "The bill provides for permanent and total disability benefits under old-age and survivors insurance, as well as under public assistance. The assistance payments will be available only to those needy disabled who either cannot qualify for insurance payments or who need supplementary aid.

The committee recommends a conservative disability insurance program to fill the present gap in the social insurance system. . . ." H. Rept. 1300, 81 Cong. 1 sess., p. 27.

The minority report recommends that total and permanent disability payments be confined to the public assistance program. The same, pp. 158-59.

The provisions governing eligibility for disability insurance reads as follows:

"Sec. 219. (b) An individual is insured for purposes of disability insurance benefits if he had not less than—

"(1) six quarters of coverage (as determined under section 213 (a) (2)) during the thirteen-quarter period which ends with the quarter in which his disability determination date occurred; and

"(2) twenty quarters of coverage during the forty-quarter period which ends with the quarter in which his disability determination date occurred. In case such individual was previously entitled to disability insurance benefits, there shall be excluded from the count of the quarters in each period specified in paragraphs (1) and (2) any quarter any part of which was included in the period of disability unless such quarter is a quarter of coverage." H.R. 6000, pp. 89-90.

[20] For the precise language see H.R. 2893, sec. 205 (a).

sions would be "too severe on newly covered workers, even if they had a few previous quarters of coverage." [21]

The objective of the proponents of the bill is to make substantial benefits under the system available about as soon as can be done, while still preserving the appearance of a contributory system. The proposed reduction in the qualifying conditions would result in a substantial windfall benefit for a person who is taken into the system in the latter part of his working life but is still young enough to qualify. He will contribute only a small part of the cost of the old-age benefit for himself and his wife (if his wife is eligible), and the bulk of the costs of his substantial benefits will be paid by taxes levied against others. Such a liberalization of the eligibility requirements would add substantially to the costs.[22]

Special provisions for women. Under the present law the age at which insured women may retire is the same

[21] Dr. Arthur J. Altmeyer, Ways and Means Committee Hearings, 1949, pp. 1164.

[22] The Ways and Means Committee did not adopt the one in four ratio recommended but adhered to the one in two of the present act. Its report on this subject reads in part:

"The extension of old-age and survivors insurance coverage to large new occupational groups requires changes in the eligibility provisions to enable members of these groups to qualify for benefits within a reasonable period of time. However, it would be undesirable if benefits could be obtained on the basis of inconsequential amounts of employment and contributions. To this end, the bill retains the provision in the present law as the basic requirement for 'fully insured status' (which entitles individuals to old-age and all type of dependents and survivors benefits). To be fully insured under this provision, an individual must have been engaged in covered employment either in approximately half his possible working lifetime after 1936 or for 10 years.

"To reduce the handicap of a late start in the case of those whose occupations will now be covered for the first time another method of becoming insured is provided which, however, is applicable to all workers. It permits an individual to be fully insured, whether in newly covered employment or not, if he has worked in employment covered by the act for approximately 5 out of the ten years immediately preceding his death or his claim for old-age benefits. The change will be especially helpful to those newly covered workers who are already old as is shown by table 5." H. Rept. 1300, 81 Cong. 1 sess., p. 25.

as that for men, 65 years. Wives and widows of insured male workers are not eligible for old-age benefits until they have attained the age of 65. H.R. 2893 would reduce the age of eligibility for women to 60 years.[23] The reduction in the age for widows and wives of primary beneficiaries is justified primarily by the fact that on the average wives are a few years younger than their husbands.[24]

Proponents of the bill deem it desirable to have a wife eligible for benefits if the husband retires at 65 or soon thereafter and to have a widow of from 60 to 65 eligible upon the death of the husband. The additional cost which will result from the reduction of the age for women is estimated to be over four tenths of one per cent of covered pay roll in 1980 according to the low-cost estimate and over six tenths of one per cent according to the high-cost estimate.[25]

The present law contains a number of discriminations against the women workers. They pay the same rate of tax as do the men, but as a rule they cost the fund less because they are less likely to occasion the payment of benefits for survivors or dependents. The married woman worker who retires and has a husband who has also retired on a benefit from the system gets in effect either her own primary benefit or the benefit coming to her through her husband, whichever is the greater. She cannot draw both. Eligibility at 60 would tend to offset the discrimination. H.R. 2893 also provides "Disabled Husband's Insurance Benefits" and "Disabled Widower's Insurance Benefits," which would further reduce the discrimination against mar-

---

23 Sec. 201 (a).

24 See Ways and Means Committee Hearings, 1949, p. 1191 for the statistics.

25 Robert J. Myers and E. A. Rasor, *Long-Range Cost Estimates for Expanded Coverage and Liberalized Benefits Proposed to the Old-Age and Survivors Insurance System by H.R. 2893*, Social Security Administration, Actuarial Study 28 (February 1949), p. 17. Hereafter cited as Actuarial Study 28.

ried women workers.[26] Nevertheless, these changes would increase costs.[27]

Earnings after retirement. Under the present law old-age benefits are paid only to or on account of workers who have practically retired from gainful employment. The law permits earnings of less than $15 a month in covered employment without disqualifying for benefits. The proposed system would allow earnings of less than $50 without disqualification.[28]

Proposals to include the self-employed and to increase the earnings subject to tax to $4,800 a year give a new significance to provisions regarding permissible earnings after retirement. One of the marked advantages of self-employment is that when the worker reaches age 65 no employer is in a position to say, "You are retired under the terms of our compulsory retirement system." Farmers, lawyers, doctors, dentists, and other self-employed persons can continue to work in their accustomed pursuits as long as they feel able. If a self-employed person can earn by his efforts more than $50 a month, he cannot draw benefits from the system, although he may have paid taxes on $400 a month for years and be entitled, if he chooses

26 Sec. 201 (h) and (i).

27 H.R. 6000 does not provide benefits for disabled children, husbands, or widowers as recommended in H.R. 2893. It does not provide for the lowering of the eligibility age for women to 60. On the subject of a lowered age the committee report reads:

"Your committee carefully considered the advisability of reducing the minimum age at which old-age benefits are payable below the present age of 65. However, cost considerations make any such change inadvisable. For instance, the life expectancy at age 65 is currently 12.1 years for men and 13.6 years for women, whereas at age 60 the corresponding figures are 15.1 and 17.0 years, respectively, or about 25 percent higher. Moreover, contributions would be paid for 5 years less if retirement occurred at age 60 instead of age 65.

"The addition of permanent and total disability benefits makes less necessary the lowering of the minimum age for old-age benefits. Many of those in need of earlier benefits than at age 65 will qualify under these provisions." H. Rept. 1300, 81 Cong. 1 sess., pp. 23-24.

28 H.R. 2893, sec. 206 (b) (1).

to retire, to draw a primary benefit of substantially more than $50 and a wife's benefit of over $25—if he has an eligible wife.

Private voluntary annuity contracts and a considerable number of retirement systems provide either (1) that payment of the annuity begins at the specified age, whether or not the insured retires, or (2) that if retirement is deferred after the specified age the amount of annuity to be paid on actual retirement is substantially increased. The present value, or the cost of an annuity of $50 a month, drops rapidly as retirement is deferred. Under voluntary systems, the individual can adjust his affairs to meet his own requirements. An annuity beginning at age 65 may be used by the self-employed to offset diminished earnings or to permit some reduction in the intensity of work. Deferring payment of the annuity to a later age reduces the disparity between former earnings and income after retirement. Either alternative leaves a substantial incentive for continuing to work, which may be in the interest both of the individual and his family. To an increasing degree it is being recognized that for many men and women continued work and earning give greater satisfaction than retirement. With the gradual aging of the population, it will become increasingly important that men who have made a success of self-employment continue working as long as they choose.

Provisions penalizing earnings after retirement may diminish the productivity of the nation and increase the cost of old-age and survivors insurance. It may discourage self-support and continued activity after age 65. As the population ages, it may become increasingly desirable for the older persons to continue working to enhance productive capacity. Government action to put a premium on retirement is justified only when imperfect functioning of the economy produces temporarily a labor surplus. The objective of the government should be to encourage the creation of suitable work for its older citizens rather than to induce them to retire.[29]

COSTS OF THE PROPOSED SYSTEM

In the preceding pages the major proposed changes from the existing law have been briefly described and their influence on costs discussed. No one can predict with even approximate accuracy the cost of an old-age, survivors, and disability insurance system such as that proposed in H.R. 2893. The difficulty arises from the number of variables that determine cost.[30] Some of them partake of the nature of natural forces with respect to which fair predictions can be made on the basis of the past. Others are economic and political; and those who have assayed long-run economic and political forecasting have not achieved successes that gain wide acceptance of their conclusions. A brief enumeration of the variables, very roughly classified as natural and as economic and political, will suggest the difficulty of estimating.

Major natural forces affecting cost are: (1) the mortality rate, (2) the birth rate, (3) the marriage rate, (4) the disability rate, with distinctions as to temporary, permanent, total, and partial, and (5) the age distribution of the population.

These five factors have to be measured with differentiation by sex, race, and age, and often also by marital status.

---

29 H.R. 6000 does not tax or compute benefits on earnings in excess of $3,600 nor does it apply to farmers and private practitioners of the leading professions. Thus it avoids much of the criticism which could be directed against the provisions recommended in H.R. 2893.

It raises permissible earnings from the present $15 limit to the recommended $50 limit for retired persons under 75 years of age. After age 75 all limits are removed.

Obviously distinguishing between earnings of the self-employed and returns resulting from ownership of a business will present substantial administrative difficulties. See H. Rept. 1300, 81 Cong. 1 sess., p. 25, for some of the suggested criteria.

30 For the technical aspects of the subject see Social Security Administration, Actuarial Study 21.

Major economic and political factors affecting cost are: (1) levels of earnings, (2) the distribution by rates of earnings, (3) levels of prices and living costs, (4) the extent and duration of employment, and (5) the propensity to retire on benefits when eligible.

In the past these economic factors have been profoundly affected by booms and depressions, which often have been related to general world conditions, both economic and political. Booms and depressions have, moreover, affected the birth rate and the marriage rate; and it may be assumed that in an insurance system they will have a marked effect on the disability rate as measured by the number drawing disability benefits.[31]

The table on page 27 estimates what the system under H.R. 2893 would cost. On the basis of two sets of assumptions, the actuarial division of the Social Security Administration has made two estimates—one a low-cost estimate and the other a high-cost estimate. Both series of estimates assume that the level of earnings of a year or so ago will prevail throughout the period. No one expects the level of earnings to remain constant, but such figures are more useful than would be others based on assumptions as to what earnings will be in the future.[32] For example, experience shows that an increase in money earnings resulting from an upward swing in prices and the cost of living will create a political demand for changes in the benefit formula—hence the estimates of cost would not be very revealing. It should also be noted that *these estimates do not include the cost of the weekly disability benefits provided for in the bill.* The number of beneficiaries, the absolute cost of the benefits, and costs as a percentage of pay roll are given by ten-year periods from 1960 to 2000, according to the low- and the high-cost estimates.

---

[31] It was the depression of the thirties that upset the calculations of the insurance companies with respect to the cost of disability insurance.

[32] Social Security Administration, Actuarial Study 28, p. 3.

BENEFICIARIES AND COSTS UNDER H.R. 2893 [a]

Calendar Year	Number of Beneficiaries (In thousands)		Absolute Benefit Costs (In millions)		Cost as a Percentage of Pay Roll	
	Low Cost	High Cost	Low Cost	High Cost	Low Cost	High Cost
1960............	7,873	12,311	$4,655	$7,163	3.21	4.92
1970............	11,758	17,671	7,536	10,914	4.82	6.96
1980............	14,993	22,801	10,065	14,688	6.09	9.05
1990............	17,741	27,650	12,150	18,270	6.92	11.02
2000............	19,160	30,666	13,236	20,604	7.07	12.40

[a] Data from Social Security Administration, Actuarial Study 28, pp. 11, 16, 17.

The most striking fact brought out by the table is the tremendous increase over the years in the benefit costs of such a program. For 1960 the range in aggregate benefit costs is from 4.7 to 7.2 billion dollars. For the year 2000 the range is 13.2 to 20.6 billions. Expressed as a percentage of pay roll, the cost in 1960 would range from 3.21 to 4.92 per cent. In other words, $3.21 to $4.92 out of every $100 would pay for the benefit costs. By the year 2000 the corresponding figures would be $7.07 to $12.40 for every $100 of pay roll.

In 1960 the number of beneficiaries under the system is estimated to range between 7.9 and 12.3 millions. The number will increase each year until by 2000 it will range from 19.2 to 30.7 millions. According to the low estimates, not quite one person in ten will be a beneficiary of the system. According to the high estimates, more than one person in six will be a beneficiary.[33]

The benefits provided by the proposed system may be classified under three heads: (1) old-age, (2) survivors, and (3) disability, excluding weekly disability benefits. The costs of these three classes of benefits expressed as a percentage of pay roll are shown in a table on page 28; both the high-cost and the low-cost official estimates are included.

[33] For population figures, see Social Security Administration, Actuarial Study 28, p. 5.

SUMMARY OF RELATIVE COSTS FOR H.R. 2893
By Type of Benefit, Excluding Weekly Disability Benefits a

(In percentages of pay roll)

Calendar Year	Total		Old-Age		Survivors		Disability	
	Low Cost	High Cost	Low Cost	High Cost	Low Cost	High Cost	Low Cost	High Cost
1960............	3.21	4.92	1.56	2.88	1.35	1.25	.30	.79
1970............	4.82	6.96	2.41	4.26	1.98	1.70	.42	1.00
1980............	6.09	9.05	3.24	5.92	2.39	2.04	.46	1.09
1990............	6.92	11.02	3.93	7.73	2.53	2.18	.47	1.10
2000............	7.07	12.40	4.14	9.04	2.45	2.18	.49	1.18

a Data from Social Security Administration, Actuarial Study 28, p. 15.

These figures indicate that the old-age benefits are the most costly and the survivors benefits are second. Disability benefits appear to be relatively inexpensive, costing in the year 2000 only 49 cents per $100 of pay roll according to the low-cost estimates, and $1.18 according to the high-cost. It should be remembered, however, that data for estimating disability costs are not very satisfactory, and it is possible that disability costs will run substantially above the high figures.

Benefit payments account for the major share of costs in the old-age and survivors insurance system. Administrative costs constitute the second and a relatively minor portion. Under this system the government must (1) collect the earmarked special taxes, (2) determine who is eligible to receive benefits, (3) make benefit payments, (4) maintain a complete record of the earnings of each individual in covered employment from the time of his entrance to the time of his retirement or death in the active service, and (5) supply covered employees with information as to their status and payment. Basing benefits on earnings involves maintaining an elaborate system of wage records and supplying covered workers with information, and accounts to a substantial degree for the high costs of administration. The estimates for administrative costs, excluding those for weekly disability benefits, are as follows:

ADMINISTRATIVE COSTS OF H.R. 2983 a
(In millions of dollars)

Calendar Year	Low Cost	High Cost
1960	113	189
1970	162	263
1980	204	337
1990	240	406
2000	260	450

ᵃ Data are from Social Security Administration, Actuarial Study 28, p. 19.

The table below, taken from the Ways and Means Committee Report, shows the estimated costs under H.R. 6000, as compared with the present system in actual amounts and in percentage terms. It will be noted that a single figure is used instead of the usual low cost and high cost.

The amounts of the benefit payments under H.R. 6000, according to these estimates, run in general a little less than twice those required under the present act. For 1960 and 1970, however, they are more than twice as high. In

COST OF BENEFIT PAYMENTS UNDER EXISTING LAW AND UNDER H.R. 6000 a
Preliminary Estimate

Calendar Year	In Percentage of Pay Roll		Amount (In billions)	
	Existing Law	H.R. 6000	Existing Law	H.R. 6000
1950	0.9	1.1	$0.7	$1.3
1955	1.6	2.2	1.4	2.6
1960	2.1	3.2	1.8	3.8
1970	3.1	4.8	2.9	6.2
1980	4.3	6.2	4.3	8.4
1990	5.5	7.6	5.8	10.6
2000	6.2	8.1	6.8	11.7
Level premium:				
At 2 per cent interest	4.45	6.20	—	—
At 2¼ per cent interest	4.35	6.05	—	—

a H. Rept. 1300, 81 Cong., 1 sess., p. 34. These figures are preliminary and subject to change. They represent an intermediate estimate which is subject to a significant range because of the possible variation in the cost factors involved in the future.

1960 benefits would be 1.8 billion dollars under the present act and 3.8 billions under the new bill; comparable estimates for 1970 are 2.9 billions and 6.2 billions.

The figure for the year 2000 under H.R. 6000 is 11.7 billion dollars, which may be compared with 13 to 21 billion dollars under H.R. 2893. The benefit costs as a percentage of pay roll in the year 2000 are 8.1 under H.R. 6000 as compared with 7.07 to 12.40 under H.R. 2893.

A table reproduced below shows the costs of the several benefits under H.R. 6000, expressed as percentages of pay roll.

ANNUAL COSTS OF H.R. 6000 (PRELIMINARY ESTIMATE) BY TYPE OF BENEFIT
(As percentages of pay roll) a

Calendar Year	Old Age	Dis- ability	Wife's	Wid- ow's	Par- ent's	Child's	Moth- er's	Lump Sum	Total
1950	0.6	—	0.1	0.1	b	0.2	b	0.1	1.1
1955	1.0	0.2	.2	.3	b	.4	0.1	.1	2.2
1960	1.5	.4	.3	.5	b	.4	.1	.1	3.2
1970	2.4	.6	.4	.9	b	.4	.1	.1	4.8
1980	3.5	.6	.4	1.1	b	.4	.1	.1	6.2
1990	4.7	.6	.5	1.2	b	.4	.1	.1	7.6
2000	5.3	.6	.5	1.2	b	.3	.1	.1	8.1
Level premium at 2 per cent interest	3.7	.5	.4	1.0	b	.4	.1	.1	6.2

a H. Rept. 1300, 81 Cong. 1 sess., p. 35. These figures are preliminary and subject to change. They represent an intermediate estimate which is subject to a significant range because of the possible variation in the cost factors involved in the future.

b Less than 0.05 per cent.

CHAPTER II

UNEMPLOYMENT COMPENSATION

Among the several programs that together constitute a social security system, unemployment compensation is the most difficult to consider from the standpoint of cost. Biological forces play an important role in determining costs of insurance to give protection from disability, sickness, old age, and death. The action of these forces can be recorded, and forecasts for the future can be based on the resulting statistics with a reasonable degree of assurance. On the other hand, scientific forecasts of the costs of unemployment compensation on the basis of past experience are impossible. This is because the forces that determine the cost of unemployment compensation are economic and political and change with the shifting tides in business and politics. This chapter will outline the present system and our experience with it, and will briefly consider certain factors and pressures which will have an important bearing on future costs. The details of financing will be taken up in Chapter IX.

THE PRESENT SYSTEM

Unemployment compensation has not been developed by the application of mathematical or actuarial principles of insurance. The approach has been empirical and experimental rather than scientific. The Congress, in adopting the Social Security Act in 1935, imposed a 3 per cent tax on the pay roll of all employers of eight or more in covered employment, on the assumption that the proceeds of such a tax would produce over the years a sufficient sum to operate a compensation system that would cushion the effect of unemployment.[1] It would not and did not attempt to provide for all unemployment. Even for covered

[1] 49 Stat. 639.

and insured employees, prolonged unemployment would have to be provided for in some other way.

Under the Constitution of the United States, as interpreted when the Social Security Act was passed, it was extremely doubtful whether the national government could legally operate an unemployment compensation system. The national act was therefore so drafted that it virtually forced the various states to adopt compensation systems that would meet the requirements of the national act. The federal tax of 3 per cent on employers of eight or more was not an earmarked special tax to finance unemployment compensation. Proceeds from this tax were covered into the treasury as general account receipts, in the same manner as all other taxes imposed for the general purposes of government. If, however, a state adopted a compensation plan that complied with the requirements of the national act, employers in that state could offset against the federal tax the amount that they paid in special state taxes earmarked for unemployment compensation up to 2.7 per cent of the federally taxed pay roll. To give the states freedom to use experience rating or individual employer's funds, the national law further provided that, if the state law used such a system, employers could offset against the federal tax their savings in the state tax that resulted from such devices up to the maximum of the 2.7 per cent.

Under this system the individual states determine several of the major factors upon which cost depends. Among them are:

1. The amount and the duration of benefit payments.
2. The conditions upon which benefits are granted including such elements as:

a. The amount of service or earnings during the base period required to establish eligibility. The states fix the base period.

b. The length of the waiting period, or the length of time an otherwise eligible person must be unemployed before he is entitled to begin to draw benefits.

c. Within limitations prescribed in the national law the acts of an otherwise eligible employee or of the union or other group of which he is a member that will disqualify him from receiving immediate benefits. The states differ with respect to the acts which disqualify and the penalty imposed for those acts.

3. Whether the system shall include experience rating and if so the system to be used.

Experience rating, it should be noted, is a factor which tends to hold down costs. For example, if an automobile company can reduce its tax by preventing unemployment, it has a great incentive to reduce to the lowest possible figure unemployment from shut-downs for retooling or from maladjustments in the flow of work or materials. The lower tax that results applies to the entire covered pay roll of the company for the year, and the savings make the extra effort worth while. Experience rating also gives management an incentive to take an interest in unemployment compensation and to help to eliminate abuses.

Experience rating and the concern of the employer with respect to administration stem from the fact that the national law levies the tax exclusively against the employer. Most states follow the same practice. The underlying conception is that most unemployment is due to causes beyond the control of individual employers, and hence the insurance costs should be borne by society as a whole. This could be accomplished by levying the tax on the employers, who would seek to pass the costs along to the consuming public in general.

PAST EXPERIENCE

Owing to increasingly favorable economic conditions since the inception of unemployment compensation, the system has not been subjected to a real test. The original law prohibited the payment of compensation "with respect to any day of unemployment occurring within two years after the first day of the first period with respect to which contributions are required."[2] The objective was to build a reserve before any compensations were paid out. All states promptly fell in line. Hardly had this two-year accumulating period expired before the United States became the arsenal of democracy and, a few years later, an active participant in the Second World War. On the one hand, employment and earnings subject to tax reached unprecedented heights; on the other hand, compensable unemployment declined to what may be regarded as minimum proportions. In this very favorable employment situation, special taxes have been more than sufficient to meet the necessary outlays.

Near the close of the War, the Administration feared that mass unemployment among civilian workers would exhaust the reserves credited to the several states—a development which failed to materialize. To care for the returned soldiers who could not quickly find satisfactory civilian employment, the government provided unemployment benefits. Consequently, in 1948 the reserves in the United States treasury credited to the states aggregated over seven billion dollars. The taxes imposed, even with experience rating deductions, have proved higher than were necessary to provide unemployment compensation under the economic conditions that have prevailed in the United States for the past decade.

In the light of this development state legislatures have generally readjusted their systems. In many states, both the amount and the duration of benefits have been increased. Additional states have adopted experience rating plans, thereby reducing the tax on employers. In states with experience ratings in one form or another, the effective tax rates have declined as more and more employers have had good records. In some states it became evident that the system was being abused—possibly by a relatively

2 49 Stat. 640.

small number of workers—and hence there was a tendency to strengthen the laws with respect to disqualifications and penalties and to adopt administrative practices designed to close loopholes.

BASIC PHILOSOPHY

The basic philosophy which the United States ultimately adopts with respect to unemployment compensation may materially influence costs. When the Social Security Act was under consideration, advocates of unemployment compensation were far from agreement as to the kind of system the nation should have. Those who believed in a national system nationally administered with a uniform tax and a single pooled fund did not develop pressure groups to support their case because of fear that, even should the Congress pass such a law, it would be held unconstitutional by the Supreme Court as then constituted. The result was that the federal act, as has been noted, gave the states a wide range of discretion for determining, in accordance with their own philosophy, the kind of system they should have. Decisions of the Supreme Court since that time have removed some of the constitutional questions, and thus advocates of nationalization are now organized to press their case.

A national system would of necessity be substantially uniform with respect to many of the factors that influence cost. Some of these factors call for brief consideration here.

Advocates of nationalization have long opposed experience rating. They maintain that the extent of unemployment in an industry is predominantly the result of factors over which the employers in that industry have little control. A basic industry, moreover, upon which others depend, such as steel or coal, may have relatively high unemployment in bad times, whereas others by their very nature have stable employment. The cost of unemployment compensation, according to this view, should be spread over all industries by a uniform tax with no deductions for favorable experience. A stable industry in competition with an unstable one would derive no tax advantage from its stability; and within an industry the employer who by careful planning had achieved stability would have no tax advantage over a competitor who had not.

Abolition of experience rating would lessen the incentives of employers to follow carefully the administrative action of the government with respect to their employees, because that action would not directly affect their tax. The practice now followed in some states of notifying an employer when his account is to be charged for compensation to some one who worked for him during the base period would presumably be abandoned. Thus the employer would no longer have either the incentive or the administrative means of checking the action of the governmental agency granting compensation.

The individual states have differed considerably with respect to what may be termed the liberality of their provisions which affect cost. Some states may have given thought to their own competitive position or to the competition for workers between employers who are "covered" and those who are not.

Legislators in rural states may not have been subject to the pressures experienced by legislators in industrial states. Under a nationalized system it may be assumed that legislators from the urbanized industrial states would be under pressure to liberalize benefits to make them satisfactory to workers confronted with high costs and levels of living. Employers in those states who had competitors in less liberal states might not be adverse to action which would increase the labor costs of their competitors. Nationalization would presumably tend toward uniformity at higher levels than the present average, thus increasing the cost of unemployment compensation at any given level of unemployment.

Under a national system uniform definition and interpretation of certain terms that may have a marked influence on cost would be anticipated. The three which will be here mentioned are: (1) leaving a job without good cause, (2) suitable employment, (3) and actively seeking work. These terms are usually broadly defined in state laws and are made more specific in regulations and in decisions on individual cases. In unemployment compensation, it should be noted, the primary examiners necessarily have wide opportunity for the exercise of discretion.

The issue with respect to leaving a job without good cause turns on whether or not the cause was occasioned by the act of the employer. If an employer gives an employee good cause for leaving, it is generally recognized that the employee is entitled to compensation for the resulting unemployment after the waiting period. If the employee quits of his own volition without good cause attributable to the employer, should he receive compensation if his reason for leaving was good? For example, an employee who is bored or discouraged in his job quits voluntarily to look for a more satisfying position, or in the belief that he had a better one lined up. The better job fails to materialize; the old job may have been filled, or the relationship of the parties may have made a return to it mutually undesirable. Women employees who have domestic responsibilities are another example of such cases, since changes in family affairs may necessitate their leaving a job, although their employers want them to stay. A borderline case of this type would be one in which the employer has to change working hours because of new shift arrangements, and the new hours are not feasible for the woman employee. Should the unemployment resulting from such changes be compensated? Obviously, the decisions on these points will affect costs, especially since, in the absence of strict administration, they permit abuses.

Suitable employment presents similar difficulties that

have been accentuated during the postwar readjustment. For substantial numbers of workers, particularly women, the war made available relatively high-grade jobs at good wages, despite lack of qualifications which in more normal times would have been required. After the war, changes in the supply and demand for workers meant that many lost their attractive jobs. Naturally they sought comparable jobs, since from their point of view other less attractive jobs were not suitable. In many cases jobs were immediately available for which such workers possessed the normal entrance qualifications; often just the type of jobs they had held prior to the development of acute labor shortages. Thus in many cases there was the anomaly of persons drawing unemployment compensation when employers were actively seeking workers for positions that they had held before the war and for which they were qualified.

Suitability of a job is closely related to the requirement that the recipient of compensation shall be actively seeking work. Employers may contend that a worker is not actively seeking work if he turns down offers of jobs of the type he filled before the war emergency. The employee may allege that he is actively seeking work, even if it is generally recognized that there are practically no prospects of a job of the type he would deem suitable. Since compensation benefits in some cases about equal net earnings after taxes and job expenses, the recipient may be under no great pressure to get another job until his benefits are exhausted. In extreme cases, particularly among married women, the facts appear to be that the beneficiary will leave the labor market unless a particularly attractive job which meets her personal requirements happens to develop. In other extreme cases, the beneficiary may be actually employed in uncovered occupations, yet draws compensation because ostensibly seeking suitable work in a covered occupation.

The cost of unemployment compensation will be affected by the law and the regulations defining such terms and perhaps even more by the application of these terms in individual cases. Relatively low costs will occur if compensation is paid only when unemployment results from defects and friction in the operation of the economic system or from the specific actions of the employers. They will increase as the system relieves the individual worker from pressures to hold on to his place on a pay roll, or, if he is unemployed, to get back on one as soon as he can get a job that will maintain him and his dependents, although it is not suitable in the sense of being desirable or of preserving prestige.

Penalties for faults are also a factor in costs. In some states conduct that is improper under the law may result in no benefits for any of the unemployment connected with the improper conduct. As a further penalty the rights to compensation for subsequent unemployment in the benefit year may be curtailed. The liberal philosophy would restrict penalties as a rule to extensions of the waiting period. If the employee remained unemployed during the extended waiting period, he would thereafter be entitled to full benefit for the duration allowed by law, should he remain unemployed that long.

Some advocates of liberality would apply this type of penalty in the event of unemployment due to labor disputes to which the employee is a party in interest. In many states the employee is not eligible for compensation for unemployment resulting from a labor dispute to which he or the organization to which he belongs is a party, no matter how long the dispute may last. Under the extreme philosophy, compensation would be payable after the prescribed penalty waiting period in full amount and for the full duration of the benefit period to which each individual is entitled, if the strike should last that long. The union would have to finance its striking members only for the penalty waiting period. The dependents of the strikers would be taken care of from the proceeds of taxation. Large and prolonged labor disputes under such a system would make heavy drafts on compensation funds.

Unemployment compensation thus lies in the controversial field of the relationships between labor and management. Under the national act the tax to force the states into line is levied against the employers exclusively, and in most states the employers pay the whole tax. The theory was that the cost of unemployment should be regarded as a cost of production and should ultimately be paid by the consumers of the product. The simple device was to levy a tax on the pay roll of the employer so that the tax would become part of his labor costs. In the long run employers would have to recover their production costs from purchasers of their product.

This method of financing gives employers the argument that since they pay the whole cost, the system should not provide benefits that are against what they regard as their immediate interests. Should the legislators decide that compensation ought to be paid while a person waits for the job he wants at a time when the economic system as a whole is experiencing a shortage of man power, then the use of some other form of taxes would be justified, at least in part. Recognizing the persuasiveness of this argument, some proponents of the extreme philosophy suggest that a tax on the pay of the employees should be introduced in the system, particularly if it is nationalized. Employees would then be in a position to say that since they were paying half the taxes they were entitled to benefits that are in their social and economic interest, although not in the immediate interest of employers.

From a financial standpoint the unemployment compensation system is not based on actuarial principles. The approach, as was pointed out at the beginning of the chapter, was to have the states experiment with what they thought they could do with the proceeds of a 2.7 per cent tax on covered pay roll collected annually but subject to such deductions as might be allowed under an experience rating system. Excess of receipts over compensation payments builds up the reserve fund, and if payments exceed receipts, the reserve is reduced. The effective tax rate and its yield are sometimes used as indicating long-run average annual costs, but there is no assurance that receipts will balance expenditures. Favorable balances and a strong reserve encourage liberalization of the system and a reduction in effective taxes. Liberalization through legislation and administration means higher costs at any level of unemployment, and tremendous costs in event of a prolonged and severe recession.

The point is sometimes made that in the event of a severe and prolonged recession, the cost of unemployment compensation will reach a maximum and then decline. This phenomenon, it is alleged, would result because many insured workers would exhaust their benefit rights and acquire no new ones until business conditions and employment improved. This hypothesis involves an assumption that in a depression legislators would not change the duration of benefits but would immediately adopt some other device to provide for unemployed employables. The assumption seems unrealistic. More likely legislators would amend the law, and the costs of unemployment compensation would continue to rise until substitute devices for providing for the unemployed were developed or until the economy again turned upward. The cost of unemployment and of unemployment compensation is unpredictable. Financing the costs will be taken up in Chapter IX.

CHAPTER III

MEDICAL CARE

Up to the present the national government has adopted no legislation providing personal medical care for all citizens. It has for years supplied such care for certain groups, notably members of the armed services, veterans, and Indians living on reservations. The great body of American citizens have obtained medical care, either through private arrangements or through state, local, or philanthropic institutions—often through a combination of the two.

For several years bills have been introduced in the Congress providing for some participation by the national government in the field of personal medical care. These bills may be divided into two broad classes: (1) those that would establish almost all-inclusive compulsory health insurance; and (2) those that would make federal grants-in-aid to the states to encourage and help them in developing comprehensive plans for providing adequate personal medical services for those who lack the resources to pay for them either in whole or in part.

The present chapter is primarily concerned with the costs of such programs. Since no data are in existence that permit reasonably accurate forecasts of costs, the discussion will be devoted mainly to the factors which will have have great weight in influencing costs.

The costs to be considered are those which the government would assume and which would necessitate payments from public funds. In part the proposals would transfer to the government costs now paid by individuals and private agencies. To some extent they would result in payment in full for services now rendered without charge or without full charge. To an unknown degree they would lead to furnishing personal medical care where it is not given at all and to an increase in the nature, extent, and duration of that at present provided. Cost factors will be considered first for compulsory health insurance and then for grants-in-aid.

COMPULSORY HEALTH INSURANCE

Enactment of an almost universal compulsory health insurance law would transfer from the private to the public sectors of the economy a high percentage of the costs of personal medical care. Expenditures now made by individuals and families for their own care would be profoundly affected. In 1948 personal expenditures for medical care and related items amounted to about 7.4 billion dollars.[1] The disposable money income of the people of the United States was about 202 billion dollars.[2] Thus 3.7 per cent of the disposable money income went for personal expenditures for medical care and related services. This is equal to an annual per-capita personal payment for medical services of a little over $51.[3] The expenditures and capital outlays made by philanthropic individuals and nonprofit private agencies in furnishing medical care and medical facilities would also be affected.[4]

Not all present expenditures would be immediately transferred to the public sector of the economy. Some persons would continue to pay part or all of the costs of their care. Estimates showing the degree of transfer—both immediate and ultimate—have been prepared by Dr. I. S. Falk.[5] His

[1] *Survey of Current Business* (July 1949), p. 23. Free services or services at less than cost do not occasion payments by individuals and families and hence are not counted in private payments by individuals or families.

[2] Derived from data on national income, the same, pp. 10-25.

[3] The estimated population of the United States on July 1, 1948 was 146.1 millions exclusive of persons in the armed forces overseas, who presumably spent little personal income for this purpose. U. S. Bureau of the Census, *Current Population Reports, Population Estimates*, Series P-25, No. 15, Oct. 10, 1948, p. 7.

[4] State and local governments, it may be assumed, would discontinue the activities that relate to the provision of personal medical care and facilities, when the national governmental system becomes effective. In many instances their facilities would doubtless be absorbed by the national system.

[5] These estimates have been published under the title "Cost Estimates for National Health Insurance, 1948," *Social Security Bulletin* (August 1949).

estimates indicate that the initial cost of compulsory health insurance would be $37.29 per capita, but that the cost would increase to $50.47 as the system is perfected. The details of these estimates are presented in the tables on pages 45 and 46.

These transfers to the public sector would be effected under a system revolutionizing methods of paying for personal medical care. Under current proposals taxes on earnings or pay—not in excess of a specified amount, say $4,800 [6] —would be levied against employers, employees, and self-employed without exemptions and the government would itself contribute from general revenues.[7] All who had contributed through taxes in the amount and for the time necessary to acquire an insured status would get—without further payment—the services provided by the insurance system for themselves and their dependents.

In theory, and insofar as it might prove to be administratively feasible, all insured individuals and their dependents would be entitled to the same quality and quantity of services under like conditions. If for any reason an insured individual did not care to avail himself of the services offered by the system, he would be free to obtain other services entirely at his own expense.[8] He could not avoid

[6] The figure proposed for old-age and survivors insurance in H.R. 2893 also used in the current compulsory health bill, S. 1679.

[7] The current bill for compulsory health insurance does not provide for a tax. Provision of a tax would necessitate reference of the bill to the Senate Finance Committee. The tax that is assumed is 3 per cent, with an additional contribution of 1 per cent by the government, or a total of 4 per cent. Employers and employees would each contribute 1.5 per cent and the self-employed 2.25 per cent. The amount raised by such financing would be in the neighborhood of 5.6 billion dollars. *National Health Program, 1949,* Hearings before the Senate Committee on Labor and Public Welfare, 81 Cong. 1 sess. Testimony of J. Donald Kingsley, Acting Federal Security Administrator, p. 102.

[8] Members of some religious faiths do not believe in orthodox medical services; others prefer to obtain them through facilities provided by their churches. Some persons—a substantial number—are "cultists" and have little or no confidence in orthodox medical practices. These persons would pay the tax. Whether the insurance system should provide them with the services in which they have faith would present difficult legislative and administrative issues.

PER-CAPITA PRIVATE EXPENDITURES FOR MEDICAL CARE COMPARED WITH ESTIMATED EXPENDITURES UNDER NATIONAL HEALTH INSURANCE, 1948 [a]

Estimates are at 1948 Price and Income Levels

Item	Personal Consumption Expenditures, Total Population		Per-Capita Expenditures (estimated) Under Health Insurance		Ratio of Health Insurance Estimates to Actual Expenditures Per Capita	
	Total [b] (In millions)	Per Capita	Initial or Early Year	195X	Initial or Early Year	195X
Total	$7,157 [e][d]	$49.35	$37.29	$50.47	75.5	102.2
Physicians' services	2,141	14.77	18.22	20.23	123.4	137.0
Hospital services	1,764 [d]	12.17	10.77	13.99	88.5	115.0
Dental services	864	5.96	3.75	8.93	62.9	149.8
Nursing services	200	1.38	.63	1.54	45.7	111.6
Medicines, appliances, and laboratory	1,807	12.46	3.80	4.79	30.5	38.4
1. Drug preparations and sundries	1,391	9.59	.81	1.21	8.4	12.7
2. Ophthalmic products and orthopedic appliances	416	2.87	1.78	1.79	62.0	62.4
3. Laboratory	e	e	1.21	1.79	—	—
Osteopathic physicians, chiropodists, and podiatrists, chiropractors, and miscellaneous healing and curing professions	273	1.88	—	—	—	—
Net payments (overhead and unexpended balance) to:						
1. Group hospitalization and health associations	88	.60	—	—	—	—
2. Accident and health insurance, mutual accident and sick benefit associations [f]	157	1.08	—	—	—	—
Student medical fees	3	.02	—	—	—	—
Research	—	—	.12	.99	—	—

[a] Private expenditures are based on Department of Commerce statistics. Estimated expenditures are from I. S. Falk, "Cost Estimates for National Health Insurance," *Social Security Bulletin* (August 1949), p. 9.
[b] Data from Department of Commerce, *Survey of Current Business* (July 1949), p. 23.
[c] Excludes 140 million dollars for medical care payments under workmen's compensation.
[d] Includes 200 million dollars (not in the source data) estimated to have been spent by patients for services in nonfederal governmental hospitals (general and special.)
[e] Included in this series under either physicians or hospitals.
[f] Reduces to one third the amount shown in the *Survey of Current Business* to omit estimated administrative expenses for cash sickness (wage loss) indemnity, death benefits, etc., which are included in the published figures but have no comparable representation in the estimated costs of health insurance.

the taxes by "contracting out." If he desired services over and above those offered, he would have to pay at least the extra cost.

ILLUSTRATIVE HEALTH INSURANCE COSTS AT 1948 PRICE AND INCOME LEVELS [a]
Assumed coverage: members of labor force and their dependents—
about 125 million persons

Item	Amount (In billions)		Percentage Distribution	
	Initial or Early Year	195X	Initial or Early Year	195X
Total	$4.66	$6.31	100.0	100.0
Physicians' services	2.28	2.53	48.9	40.1
Hospital services	1.35	1.75	29.0	27.7
Dental care	.47	1.12	10.1	17.7
Home nursing	.08	.19	1.7	3.1
Laboratory, medicines, and appliances....	.47	.60	10.1	9.5
Research and education	.01	.12	0.2	1.9

[a] I. S. Falk, "Cost Estimates for National Health Insurance," *Social Security Bulletin* (August 1949), p. 6. For underlying assumptions and premises, see the text and *Medical Care Insurance: A Social Insurance Program for Personal Health Services,* Report from the Bureau of Research and Statistics, Social Security Board, to the Senate Committee on Education and Labor, Committee Print 5, 79 Cong. 2 sess., July 8, 1946. Estimates in table include administrative costs.

This change in method of payment would introduce new factors that over the years would radically affect costs. The major ones will be considered under the headings (1) the influence of insurance, (2) methods of compensating practitioners and institutions, (3) administrative costs, and (4) the transfer of costs from the insurance fund to other government appropriations which would be met from general revenues.[9]

The influence of insurance. Under compulsory health insurance neither patient nor practitioner would need to give any thought to cost. Insofar as service is furnished persons who have refrained from obtaining needed services because of cost, the additional cost could be viewed

[9] During the first few years costs might possibly be held down by the absence of professional services and facilities, although it is probable that both would at once be used to capacity and perhaps beyond efficient capacity.

as warranted.[10] Unfortunately, thousands would demand services for minor or even imaginary ailments. Their demands might "dilute" the professional services available to those who really need them. Costs would increase enormously; this has been the experience wherever compulsory insurance has been introduced.[11]

Under a compulsory program, practitioners would be relieved of the necessity of giving attention to the ability of the patient to pay. If the patient could draw sick pay or temporary disability benefits, the practitioner could prescribe long periods of hospitalization or complete rest. Expensive tests and treatments could be given freely, though formerly provided only where the need for them was clearly indicated or where the patient had ample capacity to pay. Expensive alternatives might be preferred by the patient to the less expensive, although the less expensive would be adequate and would be chosen if he himself had to pay. For this reason, nations with compulsory health insurance systems have commonly found it necessary to establish strict rules governing the practitioners in their use of materials and methods. Under the British dental system, for example, the dentist can do certain minimum things in his discretion, but if he proposes to do more extensive or expensive work, he must get the advance approval of a regulatory agency.[12]

Methods of compensating practitioners. Under compulsory health insurance any one of three methods may be used in compensating practitioners: (1) fee-for-service,

10 Those who really cannot afford it would get the needed service under a grant-in-aid system. The extra cost for real cases under insurance would arise primarily where demands of individuals and families for other things have been given a priority over medical care.

11 England and New Zealand are recent examples. For England see "Estimation of Health Services," *The Economist*, June 18, 1949, p. 1130 and for New Zealand, "Compulsory Health Insurance Costs Soar in New Zealand," *Christian Science Monitor*, Apr. 14, 1947.

12 Don W. Gullett, "The British Health Insurance Scheme through the Eyes of a Canadian Dentist," *Journal of the American Dental Association* (April 1949), pp. 530-31.

(2) per capita, and (3) salary. Fee-for-service or payment on the basis of the nature and extent of the service rendered is the method at present largely used in private practice,[13] and under compulsory health insurance it minimizes the force of the slogan "socialized medicine." Unfortunately, it is the one that is likely to produce excessive costs. For example, a person with minor or fancied ills visits the practitioner who is paid the prescribed fee for treating him. Under such circumstances few practitioners are likely to discourage unnecessary visits; some may even encourage them and continue treatments long after the patient would have been discharged if he had been paying the bills.

Per-capita payments do not encourage the practitioner to give unnecessary treatments, because he is paid a fixed sum to take care of a patient on his list for a given period. From a financial standpoint his objective is to get and retain on his roster the maximum number of patients allowed by law or regulations. Unless his roster is full and he has a waiting list, he is under pressure to keep his patients satisfied. He may have to devote much time to patients with minor or imaginary ailments who would not come if they had to pay for the service. Unnecessary calls may prevent him from giving the time required to those who really need it, but this is a factor that affects the quality of service and not the costs.

Salary, contract, or subsidy payments are the hallmark of socialized medicine. Such payments may be necessary as an adjunct in any system that has to supply medical services in sparsely settled communities. The number of persons to be served may be so small that neither a fee-for-service nor a per-capita system is feasible. Under a private medical service system dwellers in such areas know

---

[13] Within recent years there has been a large growth in hospital insurance, medical services, insurance and prepayment plans which do away with or modify the straight fee-for-service payments by individuals or families.

that they must go to the nearest trading center for medical or dental services and that if conditions are serious they will be sent to medical centers in cities large enough to support them. Under universal compulsory health insurance such persons will naturally take the position that since they have paid the tax they are entitled to local services similar to that given to dwellers in larger communities. Politically, the government administrators will have to give substantial recognition to their demands, although the arrangement may not represent the best utilization of available professional personnel, and assignments to such areas may not appeal to the professional interests of the highly qualified. Provision of salaried practitioners in areas which could not support them on either a fee-for-service or per-capita basis will obviously add to costs.

The salary or contract system gives the government maximum control over costs, because the government can fix rates of compensation, and personal services account for a large portion of costs. The public school teachers offer the best parallel. The practitioners can, of course, strike as school teachers have done in some instances if they regard the salaries as inadequate.

Administrative costs. A governmentally operated compulsory health insurance system, whether centralized or decentralized, will require large numbers of government employees, clerks, auditors, inspectors, and administrators. Collection of the taxes and determination of insured status and eligibility will be relatively simple and routine, although costly in the aggregate.[14] Auditing and inspecting under a fee-for-service system will be detailed and expensive if it is properly done; if it is not done well, the charges will get out of control. In either event, high costs are likely to lead to a demand for per-capita payments or

14 The costs for this part of the system will be somewhat comparable with those for old-age and survivors insurance, but some savings could be effected by combining the two enormous routines.

salaries, which will apparently be less costly to administer. On the other hand, either of these methods is likely to lead to complaints from patients or families that practitioners or institutions are lacking in interest, negligent, or incompetent. The personal behavior of the personnel will likewise be subject to complaint. The government will have to investigate, for although many of the complaints will be entirely without substance, some will be found that require disciplinary or correctional action. High administrative costs and large numbers of lay personnel are to be anticipated.[15]

Transfer of costs to other appropriations. Administrators of compulsory health insurance systems will be under pressure to reduce the apparent cost of health insurance by making other appropriations carry part of the costs, particularly those for constructing, equipping, maintaining, and operating health facilities; producing and supplying expensive medical materials; and making elaborate laboratory tests. It should be noted that the costs of the present system charged against or on account of patients could likewise be reduced if government assumed these costs,

---

[15] Dr. Falk in his "Cost Estimates for National Health Insurance, 1948," tables from which are reproduced on pp. 44 and 46, does not set out administration as a distinct cost item. Instead, "The estimates of national health insurance costs represent, in general, the product of the number of services expected to be used and the cost per unit or per man-year of service, *increased by an allowance (5-7.5 per cent) for the costs of administration additional to costs already incurred for such functions as collections of contributions and maintenance of earnings records. . . ." Social Security Bulletin* (August 1949), p. 5. (Italics supplied.)

The cost of collecting the taxes and maintaining the earnings records would have to be added to the 5 to 7.5 per cent. These percentages alone applied to 6.3 billion dollars would give costs for new government mechanisms ranging from 315 to 473 million dollars a year. It seems probable that these figures will be exceeded in actual experience.

Old-age and survivors insurance required employers at their own expense to install and maintain elaborate recording and reporting systems. Under compulsory health insurance, practitioners and facilities will doubtless be required to install and maintain far more elaborate systems than are at present in use, and professionally trained health personnel will have to devote time and nervous energy to transactions with the government. These costs do not get into the statistics of cost.

especially those that do not largely involve personnel trained in the arts of personal medical care. Such an assumption of costs offers one partial solution of the present difficulties that would not involve the high costs of governmental regulation and control of the medical professions.

The impression is widely held that the compulsory system would cost no more than is now spent by individuals for their personal care. The distribution of the cost and the methods of payment, it is argued, would be affected rather than the volume of expenditures. Yet the system is to supply everyone with adequate medical care, including those living in sparsely settled rural communities where costs will be relatively high. Earnings of practitioners are not to be radically reduced, and those of new entrants into the medical profession are to be materially increased. It is difficult to understand how all these things can be done and the relatively high additional costs of administration paid within the limits of present expenditures. Costs much higher than present expenditures are to be anticipated.

FEDERAL GRANTS-IN-AID TO THE STATES

Proposals for federal grants-in-aid to the states are designed to ensure adequate and comprehensive personal medical care for the indigent and the medically indigent. Under such plans the individual states would have a large measure of freedom in determining how the required service should be given. Many of them have already established systems that provide fairly complete coverage. Payment of public funds to privately operated institutions to compensate them for the care of patients who cannot pay in full or in part is a not unusual practice. It has the great advantage of relieving the state or the local government of the responsibility of operating the institutions, more particularly of directing and controlling the professional personnel. Over a long period the states have gradually assumed responsibility for the care and treatment of persons with disabilities requiring long hospitalization, notably the mentally ill, the tubercular, and more recently those suffering from disabling incurable diseases.

Under a grant-in-aid system, the question of immediate cost to the individual or his family is not eliminated as a factor influencing the demand for services. Frequently, the patient is required to pay such part of the costs as investigation shows is within his means. Under some systems a public or private agency makes the immediate payments to hospitals or practitioners and permits the individual to reimburse it in whole or in part through installments adjusted to his capacity to pay.[16]

If through a grant-in-aid system hospitals were reimbursed in full for the cost of treating those who cannot themselves pay in full, the hospital should be able to reduce its charges to others. Boards of trustees and administrators of nonprofit health institutions have faced a serious situation arising from high operating costs for both wages and materials. They have been under pressure to recoup part of their losses incurred in caring for patients who cannot pay in full by raising rates for all other classes, including often members of group hospital insurance organizations. It seems probable that if the costs of caring for the indigent and the medically indigent were systematically met from public funds, the charges against others who need treatment could be reduced.

The public costs of the grant-in-aid system would obviously be far less than the public costs of compulsory health insurance. Private payments plus public payments would probably be less than the public payments under compulsory health insurance because the necessity for personal payment would restrain both patients and practitioners.

---

[16] As will be noted in the chapter on Public Assistance, H.R. 6000, which has passed the House, provides for federal participation in payments made by the state welfare agencies for the medical care of eligible persons.

CHAPTER IV

PUBLIC ASSISTANCE

This chapter deals with that ancient function of government, the granting of assistance to the needy from the public treasury. Prior to 1929 the activities in this field were carried on and financed primarily by local governments. From an expenditure standpoint, public assistance was of relatively minor importance, partly because relatives were expected to provide, and in some communities because religious and charitable organizations gave assistance from private funds. Since 1929 the financing and administration of public assistance have been revolutionized. The nation now has a highly organized public assistance system resting on federal and state co-operation. This function has become an important item in federal and state, as well as in many local budgets.

The legal foundation for the present highly organized, and on old standards, costly system was laid in the Social Security Act of 1935, which provided for federal conditional grants-in-aid for public assistance.[1] The states promptly complied with the requirements of the national act with respect to organization, finance, and administration—with a few minor exceptions in some states as to particular programs. The extent to which the local governments participate in financing and administration is now determined by the state governments, in accordance with the requirements of the federal act.

The discussion of the cost of public assistance will be confined to the system that has developed under the Social Security Act. The first section will deal with the system as it stands at present, its essential elements, and expenditures under it. The second section will describe the pro-

---

[1] 49 Stat. 620. The difficult problems of the years between 1929 and 1935 are not here considered. These years are perhaps best described as years of improvising to meet the emergencies of the depression.

posals for expansion and change as embodied in H.R. 2892, a bill sponsored by the Administration. The final section will be concerned with five issues that appear to be of major concern with respect to present and future costs. They will be briefly enumerated at this point. Their nature and financial importance will emerge as the chapter develops. The issues are: (1) the use of the open-end grant-in-aid by the national government; (2) the extent to which the national government should attempt to equalize differences in the capacity of the states to pay; (3) the proposal to make need the sole criterion for eligibility; (4) the size of the allowances; and (5) the relationships and the conflicts between public assistance and the social insurance programs. At the end of the chapter a brief summary will be given of the provisions of H.R. 6000 with respect to public assistance.

THE PRESENT SYSTEM

Under the present system the federal government shares within limits in the cost of assistance given by the states to three categories of needy persons: (1) the aged, (2) the blind, and (3) dependent children who are being cared for in the homes of relatives of the degree specified by the national act. The responsibility for providing for persons who are in need from other causes remains as in the past the responsibility of the state or the local governments. State and local governments must also bear the cost of medical care of the aged, the blind, and the federally aided dependent children if such aid cannot be covered within the limits of the assistance payments in which the national government will share.

With respect to the three federally aided categories, the national government has not specifically and definitely defined need nor established the standards by which eligibility for public assistance shall be determined. The individual states have been left wide discretion for determining these standards, which are important factors in cost. Among the matters upon which the states must act either legislatively or administratively in determining need are such items as:

1. Permitted resources. Elderly people, the blind, and dependent children may be in need despite the ownership of some real or personal property or the receipt of income from sources such as pensions, annuities, or earnings from labor. The states have to determine how much property may be owned and how much income received without disqualifying the applicant or recipient. The states differ widely in their requirements.

2. Responsibility of relatives. When public assistance was locally financed and locally administered some communities made relatives bear the load, if it were borne at all, by the simple device of appropriating little or nothing for relief. Other communities operated under laws that made relatives responsible—children for their aged parents, parents for their dependent children, and possibly brothers and sisters for each other. In actual administration the law, scriptural injunctions, and local public opinion were often combined to enforce support by relatives. Divorce and desertion were not then the factors they have since become. Under the modern system the state laws or the regulations made in pursuance of them determine to what degree, if any, relatives shall be responsible. The state determines whether the existence of relatives responsible for support makes the needy person ineligible or whether assistance shall be given and the attempt made to collect from the relatives.

3. Property liens. Ownership of real property, especially if used as a home, is permitted under many state laws, whether or not relatives are responsible. Some states provide that the state shall take the property immediately or put a lien on it for the amount of assistance granted,

enforceable when the property is no longer needed by a recipient of public assistance. Such provisions often have the effect of inducing relatives to contribute to protect their interests in the property.

The federal law does not specify the amount of assistance the state shall provide in any case or upon what basis the actual allowance given shall be determined. The federal law fixes for each category a maximum allowance with respect to which the national government will contribute. If a state pays more than that maximum, it must itself pay the full cost of the excess. A state is free to pay less than the maximum, but the national government will contribute only toward what the state actually pays.

The states determine how the amount to be allowed eligible applicants shall be figured. Most states use the so-called budget deficit method. Under it state administrators determine the items necessary for a minimum health and decency standard of living—to use the terms employed in many state laws—and the cost of those items. From this budget the operating officers deduct the resources of the applicant available to meet either the total or specific items. The remainder, the budget deficit, is the amount to be granted as assistance in the particular case. In some states, often referred to as "pension philosophy states," the assumption is that in the absence of resources, an applicant is entitled to the maximum grant permitted by state law, often the maximum grant in which the federal government will share. If an applicant has resources that the state law requires to be considered in fixing allowances, they are deducted from the maximum. In a few states, notably in the South, appropriations for the three categories have been insufficient to meet the budget deficits in each case, and hence the awards are less than the budget deficits. Some states meet inadequacy of available funds partly through pro rata reductions in allowances and partly by dropping from the rolls some previously declared eligible and refusing some or all new applicants.

The maximum allowances in which the national government will share and the extent to which it will share are most easily presented in tabular form. An official table is reproduced below. Both the maximum amounts and the basis of sharing have been amended three times since the Social Security Act was passed in 1935. The table shows the original provisions and the subsequent changes. The present provisions are in the bottom line.

Under the original act, it will be noted, the federal grant on a case basis was the same percentage of the actual

PROVISIONS FOR FEDERAL PARTICIPATION OF PAYMENTS OF
PUBLIC ASSISTANCE, 1935-48

Legislation	Maximum Amounts of Individual Monthly Payments Subject to Federal Participation			Federal Share of Expenditures Within Specified Maximums	
	Old-Age Assistance and Aid to the Blind	Aid to Dependent Children		Old-Age Assistance and Aid to the Blind	Aid to Dependent Children
		First Child	Each Additional Child		
1935 Original Act..	$30	$18	$12	1/2	1/3
1939 Amendments ..	40	18	12	1/2	1/2
1946 Amendments ..	45	24	15	2/3 of First $15 (Av.) + 1/2 of the Balance	2/3 of First $9 (Av. per Child) + 1/2 of the Balance
1948 Amendments ..	50	27	18	3/4 of First $20 (Av.) + 1/2 of the Balance	3/4 of First $12 (Av. per Child) + 1/2 of the Balance

allowance, whether the allowance was very small or at the national sharing maximum. If a state, for example, allowed $10 for an old-age case it received $5.00 of the $10 from national funds, whereas if it allowed the maximum $30 it obtained $15 from the federal government. There was no element of equalization in the original provisions. In 1946 amendments were adopted that introduced an element of equalization in that states which gave low allowances secured a higher percentage of their total allowances than did states which paid benefits approaching the maximum. Under the present law, for example, a state which gives an old-age assistance allowance of $20 or less gets a federal grant of 75 per cent of its allowance. If it allows more than $20, it receives a federal grant with respect to the excess of only 50 per cent. Thus a total allowance of $50 secures a 60 per cent grant, whereas a total allowance of $20 gets a 75 per cent grant. The larger the allowance, the larger the total grant in dollars, but if the allowance exceeds $20 the percentage diminishes.

This device, it should be noted, is not dependent on the capacity of the state to pay. If a relatively poor state makes high allowances, it receives no more per case than a rich state which gives a like allowance. Similarly, a well-to-do state which is extremely conservative in the amount it allows receives just as much per case as a poor state which allows the same amount solely because in the judgment of its legislators it can afford no more.

The amount which a state will draw from the national government under this system depends on the amount it allows in individual cases and the number of cases in which it makes allowances. If the national government should prescribe and enforce uniform standards for determining eligibility and the amount of allowances, the federal payments to the states would vary with the number of eligible individuals or families and the amount required to bring them to the established level. Then it could be said that under the open-end grant system now in use federal payments to the states vary with need. Such an approach would differ radically from the present system under which each state defines need and establishes the criteria of eligibility and the amount of assistance to be allowed in individual cases. Wide differences, attributable mainly to differences in philosophy, exist between states that are fairly comparable upon a social and economic basis. Under the existing open-end grant system the states can determine to a large extent the amount of public assistance grants they will obtain from the federal treasury.

The statistics with respect to what the individual states have done upon which these statements rest are summarized in the table on page 60.

Before presenting the statistics showing the costs of this system, a brief explanation of the absence of standards for defining need and fixing the amount of benefits is desirable. The national government in the field of public assistance is proceeding under the general welfare clause of the Constitution. Through conditional grants-in-aid it makes funds available to the states to help them provide assistance. The national government has no constitutional powers to administer public assistance programs, and how far it can go in restricting the freedom of state legislatures in determining policies with respect to them is a constitutional question. It is also a practical question. Although the majority of both House and Senate have favored the present system, they might react very differently toward proposals for strict federal standards which would largely deprive the states of their policy-determining powers.

MAGNITUDE AND GROWTH OF PUBLIC ASSISTANCE PROGRAMS

Three tables are presented below to show magnitude and growth. All three present, by specific programs, official annual figures from 1936, the first year of federal grants. They embrace both federal and state expenditures, including those of the states for "general public assistance," toward which the national government does not contribute. The first table on page 61 deals with total payments; the second, on page 63, with the number of recipients; and the third, on page 63, with average monthly payments.

Total payments. In 1947 federal, state, and local payments for public assistance were just under 1.5 billion dollars. Old-age assistance (about 990 millions) and aid

PUBLIC ASSISTANCE: SIGNIFICANT INDICES BY STATES[a]

State	Amount Expended from Federal Funds per Inhabitant (1948)	Average Annual Per-Capita Income (1945-47)	Old-Age Assistance December 1948		Aid to Dependent Children Dec. 1948	
			Average Yearly Benefit [b]	Persons Aided Per 1,000 Population 65 or Over	Average Yearly Benefit Per Family [b]	Children Aided Per 1,000 Children Under 18
UNITED STATES AVERAGE	$5.56	$1,238	$504	228	$863	26
NORTHEAST						
New England						
Maine	4.97	1,082	411	159	933	28
New Hampshire	4.26	1,067	512	129	1,030	21
Vermont	5.38	1,099	419	175	638	20
Massachusetts	7.10	1,396	738	212	1,382	20
Rhode Island	4.74	1,406	519	143	979	34
Connecticut	2.74	1,563	647	99	1,202	13
Middle Atlantic						
New York	3.65	1,673	646	97	1,337	29
New Jersey	1.84	1,476	529	67	990	10
Pennsylvania	3.62	1,276	476	107	1,088	34
Other:						
Delaware	1.76	1,545	331	58	867	14
Maryland	2.56	1,380	437	81	994	24
West Virginia	4.11	933	248	190	497	43
District of Columbia	1.45	1,513	513	47	974	20
SOUTHEAST						
Virginia	1.60	1,002	235	94	530	15
North Carolina	3.09	816	245	259	479	20
South Carolina	3.98	732	290	397	421	22
Georgia	5.70	832	247	519	477	21
Florida	10.08	1,082	478	344	505	61
Kentucky	4.49	797	249	255	459	38
Tennessee	5.35	878	319	270	579	39
Alabama	5.11	776	271	463	441	28
Mississippi	4.17	601	197	439	316	22
Louisiana	11.77	842	564	791	652	50
Arkansas	5.78	693	252	439	450	35
MIDDLE STATES						
Ohio	4.68	1,360	559	193	874	13
Indiana	4.07	1,211	411	154	634	18
Illinois	5.25	1,515	506	180	1,163	24
Michigan	5.45	1,315	508	218	1,017	26
Wisconsin	4.73	1,237	489	166	1,133	19
Minnesota	6.21	1,098	551	219	834	20
Iowa	6.01	1,095	566	187	708	15
Missouri	10.48	1,127	504	310	644	47
NORTHWEST						
North Dakota	5.36	1,324	535	189	1,119	22
South Dakota	5.86	1,225	443	229	610	22
Kansas	6.21	1,149	513	203	958	21
Nebraska	6.17	1,157	499	195	1,003	19
Colorado	13.99	1,296	938	464	1,012	34
Utah	6.73	1,121	605	263	1,287	33
Montana	8.09	1,426	538	236	841	29
Wyoming	5.34	1,290	677	247	1,155	14
SOUTHWEST						
Oklahoma	16.67	858	620	593	623	73
Texas	7.95	1,026	407	493	587	16
New Mexico	7.74	952	397	340	596	49
Arizona	7.71	1,070	627	296	1,113	31
PACIFIC NORTHWEST						
Idaho	7.12	1,154	555	284	1,126	26
Oregon	4.75	1,236	570	197	1,299	16
Washington	10.31	1,373	730	349	1,212	29
PACIFIC SOUTHWEST						
California	6.59	1,575	734	251	1,338	15
Nevada	5.20	1,715	648	230	c	2 c

[a] Based on *Social Security Act Amendments of 1949*. Hearings before the House Committee on Ways and Means on H.R. 2892, 81 Cong. 1 sess., Pt. 1, pp. 53, 56, 60, 1013-14.

[b] December 1948 average monthly figure multiplied by 12.

c Program administered without federal participation.

to dependent children (about 295 millions) were the major items. General assistance, the miscellaneous categories to which the federal government does not now contribute,

TOTAL PAYMENTS FOR PUBLIC ASSISTANCE, 1936-47 [a]

(In thousands)

Year	Total	Old-Age Assistance	Aid to Dependent Children	Aid to the Blind	General Assistance
1936............	$656,712	$155,241	$49,654	$12,813	$439,004
1937............	803,945	310,442	70,451	16,171	406,881
1938............	984,987	392,384	97,442	18,958	476,203
1939............	1,048,834	430,480	114,949	20,752	482,653
1940............	1,034,984	474,952	133,243	21,826	404,963
1941............	990,222	541,519	153,153	22,901	272,649
1942............	958,818	595,152	158,435	24,660	180,571
1943............	930,234	653,171	140,942	25,143	110,978
1944............	942,457	693,338	135,015	25,342	88,762
1945............	989,686	726,550	149,667	26,557	86,912
1946............	1,182,595	822,061	208,857	30,748	120,929
1947............	1,485,735	989,720	294,961	36,252	164,803

[a] Data from *Social Security Yearbook, 1947*, p. 44. Data through 1942 cover only continental United States; thereafter include Alaska and Hawaii.

amounted to just under 165 million dollars or about 11 per cent of the total. Aid to the needy blind, the most specific of the categories, accounted for only about 36 millions.

Growth is measured by figures for the turbulent years from 1936 to 1947. The first three years of this period were marked by the installation of the new programs, before real economic recovery had taken place. The next three, 1939, 1940, and 1941, were the years in which war in Europe and preparedness at home brought relatively high employment and, in some lines, labor shortages. Then came the war years, characterized by four factors affecting public assistance: (1) full civilian employment with high earnings; (2) large numbers of workers in the armed services; (3) allotments and allowances for dependents of military personnel; and (4) a rising price level partly checked by wage and price controls. High employment carried over into the postwar period with rapidly rising wages and prices. As the members of the armed services returned to civilian pursuits, allotments for their dependents ceased, but the national government furnished unemployment compensation for those who were unemployed and made provision for those who desired further education and for their dependents. The increase in the cost of living led the government to increase the maximum public assistance allowances toward which it would contribute. The improved financial position of the states resulting from curtailment of normal activities during the war and improved yields from some taxes permitted increased state appropriations for assistance.

The total payments for old-age assistance, aid to dependent children, aid to the blind, and general assistance show clearly the combined effects of these forces. Old-age assistance and aid to the blind show a consistent upward trend with the figures for each year exceeding those for the preceding year. Old-age assistance payments were about 475 million dollars in 1940. By 1947 they had more than doubled (about 990 millions).

The decline in general assistance payments is noteworthy. For every year from 1936 to 1940, inclusive, they were above 400 million dollars. Thereafter they dropped rapidly, reaching a low of 87 millions in 1945. In 1947 they had increased to 165 millions, which was still below the figure for 1942.

Number of recipients. The figures for cost are of course the product of the number of recipients multiplied by the average monthly payments. The figures for recipients show decreases for all programs during the war years. After the war, despite the high level of economic activity and the large veterans' benefits, all programs showed increases in recipients in 1946 and 1947. For all three fed-

PERSONS RECEIVING PUBLIC ASSISTANCE 1936-47[a]
(December data in thousands)

Year	Old-Age Assistance	Aid to Dependent Children		Aid to the Blind	General Assistance (Cases)
		Families	Children		
1936....................	1,106	162	404	45	1,510
1937....................	1,577	228	565	56	1,626
1938....................	1,776	280	648	67	1,631
1939....................	1,909	315	760	70	1,558
1940....................	2,066	370	891	73	1,239
1941....................	2,234	390	941	77	798
1942....................	2,227	348	849	79	460
1943....................	2,149	272	676	76	292
1944....................	2,066	254	639	72	258
1945....................	2,056	274	701	71	257
1946....................	2,196	346	885	77	315
1947....................	2,332	416	1,060	81	356

[a] Data from *Social Security Yearbook, 1947*, p. 44. Data through 1942 cover only continental United States; thereafter include Alaska and Hawaii.

erally aided programs, the number of recipients reached a new high in 1947, as is shown in the table above.

AVERAGE MONTHLY PAYMENTS FOR PUBLIC ASSISTANCE, 1936-47 [a]
(December data)

Year	Old-age Assistance	Aid to Dependent Children (Per family)	Aid to the Blind	General Assistance (Per case)
1936........................	$18.79	$29.82	$26.11	$24.13
1937........................	19.46	31.46	27.20	25.36
1938........................	19.56	31.96	25.22	25.06
1939........................	19.30	31.77	25.44	24.89
1940........................	20.26	32.38	25.38	24.28
1941........................	21.27	33.62	25.82	24.40
1942........................	23.37	36.25	26.54	25.23
1943........................	26.66	41.57	27.95	27.76
1944........................	28.43	45.58	29.31	28.77
1945........................	30.88	52.05	33.52	32.72
1946........................	35.31	62.23	36.67	39.48
1947........................	37.42	63.01	39.58	42.78

[a] Data from *Social Security Yearbook, 1947*, p. 44. Data through 1942 cover only continental United States; thereafter include Alaska and Hawaii.

Average assistance payments. Average monthly assistance payments remained fairly stable in the years prior to the war as shown in the table on page 63. From 1942 on the increases were marked and consistent. For old-age assistance and aid to dependent children the payments in 1947 were more than double those in 1936.

PROPOSED CHANGES

The Administration bill, H.R. 2892, proposes several changes in the existing public assistance programs that would materially increase costs. The most important ones relate to (1) categories aided, (2) the maximum assistance allowances in which the national government will share, (3) providing equalization among the states on the basis of the average per-capita personal income of each state, and (4) stiffening the conditions upon which grants are given so that states will be under more compulsion to appropriate for all who are in need. The principle of the open-end grant is maintained. Each of these proposals will be briefly considered.

The Ways and Means Committee of the House, after full hearings on H.R. 2892, included amendments to the public assistance titles of the Social Security Act in H.R. 6000 which passed the House without amendment. As in the case of old-age and survivors insurance, it seems desirable to give major attention to the proposals made to Congress by the executive branch of the government, since they reveal the direction of administrative leadership. In this case the major recommendations will be first described and the issues discussed.

H.R. 2892 would require each state to adopt plans ''including standards directed toward enabling each needy individual to secure, through assistance and his other income and resources, the essentials of living.''[2] Under this

2 Sec. 1407 (a).

proposal need would be the sole criterion, and the cause of the need would be immaterial. So far as the national law is concerned, categories such as old age, blind, and dependent children would disappear, although the states would be free to use them if they saw fit, subject to approval of their plans by the federal administrator.

Specific provision is included to permit the payment of the cost of medical services for needy individuals outside the allowances made to them for their support. Under existing practice with respect to the three federally aided categories, a beneficiary must pay for medical services from his allowance and his own resources. If more medical services are required and provided, they must be paid for from state and local funds. Under H.R. 2892 the national government would share with the states the costs of medical care for public assistance beneficiaries.

The maximum amount of the allowance in which the federal government would share would be $50 in the case of a single individual. If there is more than one eligible individual in the same family home $50 would be the maximum for the second and $20 for each additional one.[3] Thus the maximum in which the national government would share for a family of four all eligible would be $140 per month.

The proportion in which the federal government would share would no longer be uniform for all the states, but within limits would vary according to the average percapita income of the state for the three most recent consecutive calendar years for which satisfactory data are available from the Department of Commerce—with readjustments in each even numbered year. No state, however poor, could receive from the federal government more than 75 per cent of its approved assistance payments and no state, however rich, less than 40 per cent. For a state

3 H.R. 2892, sec. 1408.

whose per-capita income exactly equals that of the continental United States as a whole at the readjustment period, the national government would contribute 55 per cent. Within the maximum and minimum limits the percentage which the state would have to pay would be "that percentage which bears the same ratio to 45 per centum as the per capita income of such State bears to the per capita income of the continental United States (excluding Alaska)." Under the bill Hawaii and Alaska would be given a federal contribution of 55 per cent. Puerto Rico and the Virgin Islands one of 75 per cent.[4]

The state plan to be approved under H.R. 2892 must "provide that all individuals wishing to make application for assistance shall have opportunity to do so, and that assistance shall be furnished promptly to all eligible individuals." The state agency must provide a fair hearing to any individual whose claim is denied or is not acted upon within a reasonable time. Determinations of eligibility and amounts of assistance must be made "on bases which, within the area served, will assure to every individual the equal protection of the laws."[5] If a state does not carry out an approved plan, the bill provides that, after hearing, the federal administrator shall make no further certifications to the secretary of the treasury for payments to such state. The refusal of the administrator to certify may relate to the plan as a whole or only to activities in which there is a failure to comply.[6]

ISSUES AFFECTING COSTS

Examination of the present system and the proposed changes leads to the conclusion that there are five major issues with respect to public assistance that will have a profound influence on cost. As presented in summary

4 Sec. 1411.
5 Sec. 1407 (a).
6 Sec. 1412.

form at the beginning of the chapter they are: (1) the use of the open-end grant-in-aid by the national government; (2) the extent to which the national government should attempt to equalize differences in the capacity of the several states to pay; (3) proposals to make need the sole criterion for eligibility; (4) the size of the allowances; and (5) the relationships and conflicts between public assistance and the social insurance programs. Each of these issues will be briefly discussed in the light of the descriptive material already given.

The open-end grant. Under the present system and the proposed changes the several states have wide discretion in determining how much they will draw from the national treasury. The more liberal their criteria of eligibility, the larger their allowances in individual cases, and the greater their appropriations for public assistance, the more they will get from the national government. What a state will receive depends and will continue to depend not upon the amount and degree of need in that state as measured by uniform standards applied objectively throughout the nation but upon the standards that the particular state chooses to adopt. The amount of need in any state obviously depends upon the standards used to define need. The higher the standards, the more need and hence the greater the cost of assistance.

The open-end grant in itself offers an inducement to some states to be liberal since the national government pays a substantial part of the cost of that liberality. The dangers of greatly increased costs from this arrangement are enormously enhanced by the growing sentiment in favor of universal noncontributory old-age pensions. Elections in the state may be won on the promise of making the public assistance program as liberal as possible and getting as much as possible from the national treasury.

Equalization on the basis of per-capita personal income. If states with low per-capita personal incomes could receive from 65 to 75 per cent of their public assistance allowances from the national government, their political leaders would be under great temptation to make liberal benefits a campaign issue. Sales taxes for general state purposes are often criticized severely, but a sales tax earmarked for public assistance may be highly popular if for every 25 cents paid 75 cents will come into the state from the national government.

Federal taxes will not constitute much of a brake on movements in some states which will enormously increase the costs of public assistance. In the low-income agricultural states, which would receive high percentage grants, relatively few people pay substantial direct federal taxes. Some federal income taxpayers who are in business in the state might favor liberality on the ground that it will bring federal money into the state and improve the situation.

A question must be raised as to whether equalization would tend to curb high-income states which tend to embrace the pension philosophy. Under H.R. 2892 no state, however high its ratio of per-capita personal income to the national average, would get less than a 40 per cent grant. Even in states with relatively high per-capita incomes, there are large numbers of voters who are not oppressed by the burden of direct federal taxation. The movement for universal pensions has, as a matter of fact, gained a firm foothold in several states where the per-capita income is substantially above the national average, such as California and Washington.

What has been said here is based on the proposal to use grants for equalization under a system that leaves the states free to determine eligibility, property allowances, relative responsibility, and the amount of allowances. Were the extent of need and the amount of allowance to be financed from public funds objectively determined by uniform standards, the question of whether equalization were used would not affect costs. Costs would be fixed and equalization would be entirely a question of how these costs would be financed. Under the proposed system equalization would constitute for the poorer states, territories, and dependencies a great temptation to increase costs.

Size of allowances. In the past, legislators, administrators, and perhaps most voters agreed to the theory that public assistance allowances should be less than working persons or families of comparable status were earning in the community. Assistance allowances, according to the view then prevailing, should offer no inducements to the recipients to prefer assistance to self-support. Today federal public assistance administrators and some legislators put the emphasis on adequacy. The state plan under H.R. 2892 must include standards directed toward enabling each needy individual to secure through assistance and his income and resources the essentials of living, yet the essentials of living are not defined.

The maximum limitations on allowances under H.R. 2892, it will be recalled, are $50 for a single beneficiary, and if there is more than one in a family home, $50 with respect to the second and $20 with respect to each additional one. In Puerto Rico, the Virgin Islands, and certain areas of the South where a living is gained from subsistence farming, it would probably be found in many cases involving large families that maximum allowances would exceed normal earnings. Being on public assistance might become economically a preferred status. The marginal worker who has a large family might be acutely aware of the fact that his family would be better off if he should desert them or be so far disabled that he and they could get an allowance on that score. In fact, in Oklahoma it was found that aid to dependent children in some cases had apparently led the father to desert in order to make the family eligible.[7]

[7] See editorial in Oklahoma City *Daily Oklahoman,* Oct. 16, 1948.

A question must be raised as to whether national social security administrators do not tend to underestimate the differences in the costs and levels of living in different sections of the United States and even between rural areas and large municipalities in the same section. The proposed maxima look very different if considered from the standpoint of Puerto Rico and the Virgin Islands than if thought of in connection with great urban centers in the industrial states. It is particularly in the rural communities with relatively low earnings that the availability of what appear to be large allowances may result in efforts to get on the assistance rolls and thus increase costs.

Need the sole criterion. It seems unquestionable that making need the sole criterion for assistance under the federal grant-in-aid plan will materially increase total expenditures. In several of the industrial states the statistics suggest that provision is being made for categories that do not occasion federal aid on a scale comparable with that for the aged, the blind, and dependent children cared for in the homes of relatives. There are some states, however, where appropriations for public assistance go mainly to the federal aid categories, since each dollar so spent brings in, roughly speaking, a comparable amount of federal money. Expenditures for unaided categories in some welfare agencies are regarded as involving the loss of federal funds.

Insofar as the increased costs result from giving assistance to genuine cases of need in the amount required for necessaries, they may be regarded as fully justified. It is probable, however, that the new proposal would be more difficult to administer and to audit since the facts would be more difficult to ascertain.

Assistance vs. the social insurances. The social insurances as thus far developed have limited coverage. Certain large classes are at present omitted, notably agricultural laborers, casual workers, domestic servants in private homes, farmers, and persons working on their own account. Many subsistence and tenant farmers and many persons classified as working on their own account have very small incomes. There are, moreover, thousands of workers in positions covered by old-age and survivors insurance who for one reason or another do not attain a permanently insured status under that program.

As was pointed out in the chapter on Old-Age, Survivors, and Disability Insurance, proposals have been made to extend the coverage under that system so that it will be virtually complete so far as occupations go. Even with wide coverage under a contributory insurance system, there are always some who do not attain an insured status that will protect them. Thus a comprehensive public assistance program is always necessary as a last line of defense. The question is how large a load will be left for the public assistance program to carry. The size of that residual load will be a significant factor in determining the cost of public assistance.

The proposals for the extension of coverage under old-age and survivors insurance, however, involve two difficulties that stem from the fact that it is contributory and contributions are related to earnings. First, the mechanics of having employers withhold pay-roll taxes from the employees now excluded from the act and of collecting from the self-employed engaged in small enterprises present real problems. Second, persons who are almost certain to be eligible for public assistance may get at least as much from the assistance program without contributions as they would from the insurances after contributions. Subsistence and tenant farmers, for example, whose annual money earnings are too small to bring them under insurance conceivably would fare as well as more successful farmers who had contributed for years. Under such circumstances the Congress may be loath to extend the compulsory contributory system to cover these groups which present administrative difficulties and many members of which may resent the taxes.

While the extension of coverage of the insurances is being debated, movements for making public assistance as nearly as possible a universal system will doubtless continue. It is of course true that an insurance system costs more for benefit payments than an assistance program. The assistance program uses the means test and pays only the sum deemed necessary to bring the resources of the beneficiary to the established level. The insurance system, on the other hand, pays benefits to all regardless of their need and the amount of benefit is not reduced because of available resources. No saving in cost results from substituting the insurance program for public assistance, but the future cost of the assistance program will depend on how much is left to it.

It seems reasonable to assume that for some years to come the costs of the public assistance programs will rise. If old-age and survivors insurance is extended to cover the occupations that yield low earnings and are now excluded, the costs of public assistance will gradually be absorbed into the still greater costs of the insurance. It will take several years for that absorption to become effective to the full degree. But even with the fully developed insurance program, substantial amounts will be required to care for those who never attain an insured status.

PUBLIC ASSISTANCE IN H. R. 6000

The two most radical proposals of H.R. 2892 were (1) to make need the sole criteria for federal participation in public assistance grants and (2) to have the amount of the federal grant depend on the average per-capita personal income of the people of the state for the three most recent consecutive years for which satisfactory data are available from the Department of Commerce. Neither of these proposals was embodied in H.R. 6000.

The Ways and Means Committee proposes to add to the Social Security Act a new title which will provide federal participation in allowances given by the states to the permanently and totally disabled. It further amends the titles relating to the aged, the blind, and dependent children so as to include medical care in behalf of eligible individuals as well as unrestricted cash payments.

. . . These expenditures for medical care, however, will be counted for purposes of a Federal contribution only to the extent that they, plus the unrestricted cash payment to the individual, do not exceed the maximum of $50 in the case of old-age assistance and aid to the blind ($30 for Puerto Rico and the Virgin Islands) and $27 or $18, as the case may be, ($18, and $12, respectively, in the case of Puerto Rico and the Virgin Islands) in the case of aid to dependent children.[8]

The act is also so amended that the federal government will share in payments to individuals who are patients in public medical institutions, with certain exceptions.

The title providing aid to dependent children is amended to permit federal participation in the allowances to the parent or other relative who is caring for the child or children. Under existing law the federal government shares only in the allowance to the children.

The Ways and Means Committee adheres to the present device of diminishing the percentage of federal participation by steps as the amount of the grant increases. The schedule it proposes is:

Old Age Assistance, Aid to the Blind, Aid to the Permanently and Totally Disabled:
    Four fifths of the first $25
    One half of the next $10
    One third of the remainder not in excess of $15
    The present maximum of $50 is retained.[9]
Aid to Dependent Children:

[8] *Social Security Act Amendments of 1949*, H. Rept. 1300, 81 Cong. 1 sess., p. 152.
[9] The same, pp. 40, 50, 54.

Four fifths of expenditures not in excess of $15 multiplied by the total number of dependent children and other individuals with respect to whom aid to dependent children is paid.

One half of the amount in excess of $15 but not in excess of $21, multiplied by the number as above.

One third of the remainder similarly multiplied.

The maximum for a single dependent child and for the relative having the child in care is $27. For each additional child the limit is $18.[10]

The Virgin Islands and Puerto Rico, as the earlier quotation showed, are separately treated, with lower maximum limitations. For old-age assistance, aid to the blind, and the totally and permanently disabled the federal government will contribute one half of allowances not in excess of $30.[11] For dependent children the federal government contributes one half of allowances up to $18 for the first child and $12 for each additional child.[12]

Under H.R. 6000 a state plan for old-age assistance, aid to dependent children, and aid to the permanently and totally disabled must provide that all individuals wishing to make application shall have opportunity to do so, and assistance shall be furnished promptly to all individuals. The requirement proposed in H.R. 2892 that determinations of eligibility for the amounts of assistance or welfare services under the plan shall be made on the basis which within the area served will assure to every individual the equal protection of the law is not included in H.R. 6000, possibly because it was deemed unnecessary under a categorical system. The open-end grant system is maintained without substantial modification.

The Committee reiterates its position that the contributory social insurances should be the main program and that the importance and cost of public assistance will diminish as insurance coverage is extended.[13] In this connection

---

10 H.R. 6000, sec. 322.
11 The same.
12 The same, sec. 322.
13 H. Rept. 1300, 81 Cong. 1 sess., pp. 37-38.

it should be noted that the problem of agricultural employees and self-employed farmers, including the subsistence and tenant farmers, is deferred for further study.[14] Expansion of public assistance payments in rural states may continue until these groups are covered but, as previously noted, on an over-all cost basis coverage through the insurances means higher benefit payments than public assistance. The question of financing will be taken up in Chapter IX.

[14] The same, p. 9.

PART II

SPECIAL GROUPS AND PROGRAMS

A study of the costs and financing of social security called for the examination of three subjects that are tangential to the main issues but should receive careful consideration in arriving at basic conclusions. These subjects are included in the present part. They are concerned with the needy, veterans' benefits, and private pension and retirement systems.

CHAPTER V

WHO ARE THE NEEDY?

The preceding chapter dealt with the public assistance programs of the existing social security system. They provide for the needy who meet the eligibility requirements established by the state of residence. Eligibility is determined through a means test administered by the state. As noted in the chapter, the states differ widely with respect both to the amount of allowances and methods of determining them and the eligibility requirements, especially on such matters as allowable resources and responsibility of relatives. They also differ in the extent to which they make provision for the poor whose need is occasioned by a cause not recognized by the Social Security Act.

The old-age and survivors insurance system, as described in Chapter II, on the other hand, provides old-age and supplementary benefits without a means test for persons who have been covered under the system for the length of time prescribed by Congress for attaining an insured status. Persons may be excluded from old-age and survivors insurance because they never worked in covered employment or did not work in it long enough to attain the insured status. Although the system is supported in part by pay-roll taxes, it is so designed that for many years to come employers and employees will have paid an extremely small fraction of the costs of the benefits which the beneficiaries of the system will receive.

The existing system thus presents the anomaly of persons who are not in need receiving substantial benefits supplied by taxes levied against others, while poor people who are in need may be ineligible for public assistance. They may fall between the two systems and be protected by neither, although they are in far more unfortunate circumstances than many receiving windfall benefits under the insurance system. This anomaly results from the adoption of the insurance concept that only those who have contributed something toward the cost of their prospective benefits should acquire an insured status. The idea is that as the coverage of the insurance system is extended the importance of the discrimination will diminish and only small numbers will be left to be cared for under means test public assistance. In the meantime, significant segments of the population do not receive the protection extended to others, a situation which does violence to the democratic concept of equality before the government and the law.

Such a situation gives rise to the question, Who are the needy? Do the available statistics relating to them suggest that assuming extension of coverage under old-age and survivors insurance and the passage of time most of them will work long enough at sufficiently high earnings to attain and maintain an insured status? Will many of them have to be provided for under means test public assistance? What is the nature of the group which at present falls between the two programs and gets the protection of neither?

Specific answers to these questions cannot be given with anything approaching precision because of the limitations of the available statistics. The purpose of this chapter is briefly to summarize the recent statistics regarding the incomes of American families and individuals not in families to show the characteristics of the needy.

Emphasis should be placed on the characteristics. Government statistics not infrequently show the distribution of families and individuals by specific income groups. But for those who have small incomes, these statistics do not show adequately who they are or why they got that way. During the depression of the thirties, when unemployment was widespread, large numbers with low incomes could be accounted for by one cause, unemployment. Low wages was another explanation. But in periods of labor shortages and relatively high wages, such as the country has experienced for the past four years, why should there still be individuals and families with very low incomes? Why in April 1948, for example, should there be a little over 8 million families and individuals with money incomes of less than $1,000?

Some of the reasons are of a purely statistical nature and mean essentially that the figures are misleading. Four of them are of sufficient importance to justify explanation.

1. Income or resources are of four major types: (a) money income, (b) income in kind, (c) gifts from relatives and friends, and (d) free services from public or private sources. The simplest procedure, statistically, is to restrict an inquiry to the money earnings of the individual or members of the family, and possibly to include money income from other regular sources. This is the method often followed. Nonmoney income, or as it is sometimes called "imputed income," is either not reported or not included in the tabulations. The use of data relating to money income alone is most misleading in the case of rural populations where the farm home and food from the farm are significant items. In urban communities failure to include the rental value of owned property often leads to a lowered classification.

2. The statistical question asked gives misleading returns in certain cases. What was your income last year may refer to either the calendar year or the preceding twelve months. Each year several million new workers enter the labor market, perhaps most of them after the close of school in May or June. In the calendar year or the twelve preceding months this group had low earnings because they actually worked only the latter part of the year. If, for example, a boy starts in September at $100 a month he earns $400 in the calendar year, but he is earning at the rate of $1,200. Next year he will move up to his proper classification if regularly employed, but other part-year workers will take his place in the statistics.

3. Persons working on their own account or paid in fees or commissions constitute a special statistical problem, especially if the nature of their work is such that they have good years and bad years. Their average income for several years is a better index of their true economic position than their income in any one year. Occasionally, a salaried worker or wage earner may have a bad year because of illness or unemployment. His low earnings in that particular year do not necessarily indicate his usual or customary level of receipts. If his difficulties are temporary, he may return to his usual level of earnings in the ensuing months. For such persons, too, annual average income for several immediately preceding years is a better index than income in a single year. The use of savings or credit may tide families over the bad months so that they are not actually reduced to the straitened circumstances that their temporary low money income would suggest.

4. The concept of the family presents serious difficulties because of variations in size and dispersion of members. Statistics of families ordinarily use the "living in one abode" criterion, which is obviously not a realistic measure of the economic position of a family whose dispersed members have a high sense of responsibility for one another. In a substantial number of instances an individual living by himself constitutes for statistical purposes a family or a spending unit. The actual money earnings or income of this one-person family may be low. It is probably true, however, that a good many of these persons are in fact members of a much larger family, although actually living apart from it. Their small earnings or money income may be supplemented by gifts, allowances, etc. from the larger family, as in the case of children just getting started for themselves away from home, or elderly parents who are supported in part by their absent children. Real families as distinct from statistical families are not necessarily broken when the younger generation sets out for itself.

Many an elderly mother lives in comfort on a very small money income of her own, because she owns the house in which she lives and is helped by children who are no longer under her roof.

Statistics based on money income in one specified year thus include in the low-income categories many who are not chronically poor and are in no sense persons in need. Obviously, youths just starting out for themselves are not to be classified as people in need on the basis of their low money incomes in the first few months. Risk bearers working on their own account are not necessarily in need because they have a lean year. Included in these low money income groups are many who will be able to attain and maintain an insured status under old-age and survivors insurance, if its coverage is extended.

There are many persons, however, who actually belong in the needy category. Some classes can be definitely recognized, although the numbers in them have not been ascertained. Among them are: (1) Persons who, because of some limitation in mentality, physical condition, or character, cannot or do not earn consistently. From the standpoint of employers they are unemployable or employable only in periods of labor shortage. (2) Elderly people, especially women, who are unemployable under existing conditions. Widows or elderly deserted wives of husbands who were never good providers are in this class. Throughout their lives their existence may have been marginal. (3) Highly important under modern conditions, the wife with small children who has been deserted by her husband and does not have within herself the ability to cope with her situation. In many such cases the family was marginal even while the husband was present in the home. The wife may have no skills that fit her for more than casual employment and her responsibilities for her children make even casual employment difficult. (4) Subsistence farmers and some tenant farmers who are attempting to wrest a living from small areas of poor land with meager equipment and little live-stock. They often lack the education and experience necessary for successful farming under modern conditions. Large families are characteristic of this group.

A fifth class might be added: persons who lack the formal education and training essential for reasonable success in many occupations.[1] Statistics in this field often show the co-existence of low income and low levels of formal education. Low levels of formal education may represent (1) lack of educational opportunities, (2) lack of financial resources to permit taking advantage of available opportunities, (3) absence of family and environmental guidance stimulus and discipline often essential for educational progress, or (4) lack of the mental qualifications requisite for acquiring knowledge and skills. Often several of these factors are combined, just as their opposites are frequently combined in cases where marked success is achieved.

Youth, it must be remembered, is the period during which formal education is normally acquired, 6 to 14 years of age for elementary, 14 to 18 for secondary, and 18 to 22 for college. Thus statistics for persons now 65 years old reflect educational conditions prevailing from 43 to 59 years ago. Even persons now 40 years of age are some 18 years removed from the upper limits of the normal period for formal education. Educational opportunities are incomparably better today than they were in the earlier years of the present century. Unfortunately, very little can be done now to improve the education and the earning capacity of those already well beyond normal school age. The nation, however, has for many years steadily improved the opportunities for those still young enough to take advantage of them.

---

[1] Some persons of marked native ability have been able to acquire knowledge and skills of high order in spite of extremely limited formal education in youth. Unfortunately, many persons without a foundation of formal education have had nothing upon which to build or through which to acquire valuable skills.

THE AVAILABLE STATISTICS

The existence of the various factors thus far discussed has long been known to persons who have attempted objective studies in fields where these factors are of great practical importance, such as in relief and social security. Most research workers, however, are disturbed by the paucity of comprehensive, regularly collected statistical data to determine the weight of the factors, and by the extent to which they must rely upon fragmentary material obtained upon a sampling basis through special studies often made to further a particular cause.

Because of previous neglect of this important area all persons concerned with these problems will welcome a study entitled, *Low-Income Families and Economic Stability—* Materials on the Problem of Low-Income Families assembled by the Staff of the Subcommittee on Low-Income Families, Joint Committee on the Economic Report.[2] It is not that the staff of the committee has initiated new and extensive special studies, but rather that it has focused attention on the problems, brought together the available material, and especially has obtained the co-operation of the Bureau of the Census in exploiting the material collected in connection with its sampling studies of the distribution of money income among United States families.

No attempt will here be made to present a thorough-going summary or analysis of the material in this report. Certain of the statistics most relevant to the cost and financing of social security will, however, be briefly presented.

Families and individuals. The Census data distinguishes sharply between "Families" and "Individuals not in families." The total for these two classes combined in 1948 was 46.7 millions, of which 8.1 millions or 17.4 per cent were individuals not in families.[3]

[2] Joint Committee Print, 81 Cong. 1 sess. (November 1949).
[3] The same, p. 9.

The lowest money income class shown in the Census figures is "Under $1,000." Of the 8.1 million units in this class, 4.1 millions or slightly more than 50 per cent were individuals not in families. The second lowest money income class is $1,000 to $2,000. Of the 7.4 million units in this money income class 1.8 million are individuals not in families. Thus of the 15.5 million units reported by the Census as having money incomes under $2,000 in 1948, about 5.9 millions or 38 per cent were individuals not in families.

The individuals not in families and with money incomes of under $2,000 are characterized by relatively high percentages of persons 65 years of age and over and of women. Of the 4.1 million individuals not in families and with money incomes under $1,000, persons 65 or over constitute not quite 40 per cent, and women make up almost 60 per cent.[4] The age and sex distribution of these individuals with money incomes under $1,000 explains in part the fact that only about 40 per cent of them were employed. Of the employed women 61 per cent were "service workers," one of the lowest paying occupations.[5]

Distribution of families by money income. A diagram, presented on page 88, shows the distribution of the 38.5 million families (excluding individuals not in families) according to their money incomes in 1948. According to these figures 4 million families or 10.6 per cent of all families had money incomes of less than $1,000 and 5.6 million families or 14.5 per cent had incomes of $1,000 to $2,000. The two income classes combined contained about one quarter of all families. Three quarters of the families had money incomes of $2,000 or more, and substantially more than half had money incomes of $3,000 or over.[6]

The figures just presented include the farm families. As the report clearly recognizes, farm families should not be

4 The same, p. 53.
5 The same, p. 54.
6 The same, p. 3.

included with nonfarm families in an objective analysis because of the difference between the two groups with respect to the significance of money income. Of the 9.6 million families with money incomes of less than $2,000 about 3.3 millions lived on farms, which leaves about 6.3 millions in urban and "rural nonfarm areas."[7]

DISTRIBUTION OF MONEY INCOME OF UNITED STATES FAMILIES, 1948 [a]

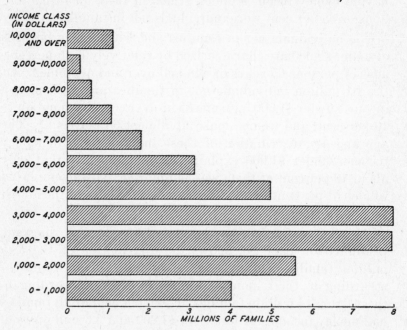

[a] Data from *Low-Income Families and Economic Stability*, Joint Committee Print, 81 Cong. 1 sess., p. 3. Does not include single-person families.

NONFARM FAMILIES

Age and low income. A total of 6.3 million nonfarm families had money incomes of less than $2,000. In more than one fourth (1.7 million) of the cases, the head of the family

[7] The same. Persons living in communities of 2,500 or over are classified by the Census as urban. People living in smaller communities but not on farms are classified as "rural nonfarm."

was a person 65 years of age or over. About half the families headed by persons 65 years of age or over had money incomes of under $2,000.[8] It must be remembered, however, that money income figures do not include the rental value of owner-occupied homes. The report brings out the fact that about two thirds of the families with money incomes under $2,000 and with heads over 65 years of age owned their homes.[9] Many may have completed payments on their homes and were therefore more fortunate in this respect than the younger home owners.

Divorced or separated women. Almost 40 per cent of the women who headed nonfarm families with money incomes of less than $1,000 a year were divorced or married but not living with their husbands. For the income class $1,000 to $2,000 the corresponding percentage was 36. Of the women who headed families with money incomes of over $3,000 a year, slightly less than 19 per cent were divorced or married but not living with their husbands.[10]

Employment of heads of families. The head of a family is the member normally regarded as responsible for supporting it. Persons under 21 years of age or over 65 are obviously handicapped as earners. The report therefore confines several tables to data for families which had heads between the ages of 21 and 64. The number of nonfarm families with money incomes of $2,000 or under and with heads between 21 and 64 was about 4.5 millions. Of this number 1.2 million or about a quarter were headed by women and 700,000 by nonwhite males.[11]

---

[8] The same, p. 4.

[9] The same, p. 27. Among families with money incomes of $3,000 or over and heads between 25 and 64 years of age, 57.4 per cent were reported as home owners; for families with money incomes of under $2,000 the corresponding figure was 43.9 per cent and for families in this income class with a white male head the figure was 49.2 per cent. The same.

[10] The same, p. 61.

[11] The term "nonwhites" is adopted from the Census report. The great majority of persons in the group are negroes but some Indians, Chinese, Japanese, and others are included.

The figures for families with money incomes under $1,000 and with heads 21 to 64 were even more striking. Slightly less than half had white male heads and about 38 per cent had women heads. By way of contrast, in similar families with money incomes of $3,000 or over more than 90 per cent were headed by white males.

A surprisingly high percentage of the women 21 to 64 years of age who were the heads of low-income families were not employed or seeking work [12] on the date of the study. For the "Under $1,000" class the percentage was 63 and for the next higher group 46. For the women 21 to 64 who headed families with money incomes of $3,000 or over, 41 per cent were not in the labor force.[13]

The heads of the low-income families who were 21 to 64 years of age and gainfully employed were engaged mainly in occupations that are commonly low paid. The figures for women show this fact with no uncertainty. Of them 55.8 per cent were "service workers" as contrasted with only 17 per cent for the women who headed families with money incomes of over $3,000. For men the comparison is not so striking because their occupations were more diverse. The percentage of male white heads employed as laborers was, however, 16.4 for the low money income families as contrasted with only 3.5 for the families with money incomes of $3,000 or over. Among the low money income families with employed nonwhite male heads, 36 per cent of the heads were employed as laborers, 20.3 per cent as service workers, and 25 per cent as operatives. Thus, these three classes of occupations accounted for 81.3 per cent of the nonwhite heads of low-income families 21 to 64 years of age.

The possible pitfalls in statistics of this type are indicated by the fact that white male heads (21 to 64) of low-income families are reported in substantial proportions as proprietors (16.0 per cent) and professional and semi-profes-

12 The Census term is "Not in the labor force."
13 Joint Committee Print, 81 Cong. 1 sess., p. 63.

sional workers, managers, and officials (5.8 per cent).[14] The figures also show that 7.2 per cent of these white male heads of low-income families had had one or more years of college and 34.2 per cent additional had had one to four years of high school. From available data one cannot tell whether the professional workers are relatively young persons just starting in their careers at the notoriously low earnings characteristic of early professional life or whether they are older persons who have encountered difficulties. Similarly, the statistics do not permit distinguishing between proprietors who had a bad year and small-scale operators who rarely make more than a meager living.

Education. The staff study contains a section on the education of the heads of low-income nonfarm families, and another on the relation between low income and lack of educational opportunity. No attempt will here be made to summarize the figures. They relate to heads of families 25 to 64 years of age and thus reflect a fairly wide span of time. Substantial improvement has taken place since the beginning of that span. American children of all classes are today getting more years of schooling and better preparation for present-day employment. It is true of course that industrial progress in the United States has enormously increased the handicap of the persons who years ago started work with very meager schooling. The statistics regarding persons now 25 to 64 years of age reflect that handicap, although they do not measure it with any degree of precision. For current purposes statistics as to what the school system is actually doing today are of far more significance.

Size of families. The low-income families are comparatively small. Of the 2.3 million nonfarm families with money incomes of less than $1,000, over 62 per cent contain only two persons. Of the 4 million nonfarm families with money incomes of $1,000 to $2,000, two-person families make

14 The same, p. 15.

up 45 per cent. Such small families constitute only 26 per cent of the nonfarm families with money incomes of $3,000 and over. Small families are to be expected where many of the heads are persons 65 or over, widowed or separated women, or persons under 21.

The figures for nonfarm families with money incomes of less than $1,000 show 270,000 families of four members and 190,000 with five or more. Thus about 20 per cent of the lowest money income families have four or more members. For nonfarm families with money incomes of $3,000 or over, the percentage with four or more members was over 45.[15] The figures do not furnish an answer to the question of how many of the low-income nonfarm families with four or more members are chronically poor and how many had a bad year. More comprehensive studies would be necessary to answer such questions.

Studies of the expenditures of low-income families generally show that a substantial percentage goes for automobile purchase and operation. The staff study contains the results of a 1948 study by the Bureau of Labor Statistics of consumer units receiving less than $2,000 of annual money income after taxes in three cities—Denver, Houston, and Detroit.[16] Here, again, are revealed substantial expenditures for automobile purchase and operation. It would be significant to know whether chronically low-income families prefer to spend their limited resources for automobile transportation or whether the automobile expenditures are made by families temporarily in the low-income group or new entrants to it. The relatively high expenditures for medical care in relation to income in these three cities suggest illness of workers as a possible explanation of low-money income in the year under study. Here again, is the question, is it temporary or chronic?

[15] The same, p. 21.
[16] The same, p. 98.

FARM FAMILIES

The significance of money income is not the same for farm families as it is for nonfarm families. The analysis of the Census data presented in the report of the staff of the Joint Committee generally treats money income of less than $1,000 as the dividing line. It thus makes allowance both for the substantial nonmoney income realized by farmers and for some understatement of true money income. Some farmers include as operating costs expenditures which reduce the expenses for living.

The data show that roughly a quarter of the 1.7 million low-income farm families are headed by persons 65 years of age or over. About 1.3 million are headed by persons 21 to 65. Of this number almost 10 per cent are women and 20 per cent nonwhite males. Nonwhite male heads of farm families between the ages of 21 and 64 number 540,000. Of this number 48 per cent had money incomes of under $1,000 and 37 per cent money incomes between $1,000 and $2,000. Only about 15 per cent had money incomes in excess of $2,000.[17]

No section of the country is free from low-income farm families, but they are most common in the South. In addition to its colored farmers the South has its white subsistence farmers, prominent among them the mountain whites. Their farms are often characterized by poor soil, small acreage, and primitive equipment. Mechanization of agriculture, if it has not lowered the condition of these groups, has at least increased the contrast between them and the successful farmers. The subsistence farmers and the tenant farmers often have inadequate resources to obtain the use of a sufficient area of good land and modern equipment. Many of them are also handicapped by the lack of the education required for successful modern agriculture.

[17] The same, p. 37.

The question should be raised as to whether subsistence farmers, and share croppers, and other poor tenant farmers will have the earnings which will permit them to attain and retain an insured status under old-age and survivors insurance. At present a high proportion of them belong in the category of the chronically poor. It is doubtful whether their fundamental problems can be solved through relief or social security.

CONCLUSIONS

The available statistics on the low-income individuals and families are obviously unrefined and in many respects inadequate. They do, however, warrant the following conclusions.

1. In the low-money income brackets are combined at least three distinct groups, each of which has a different relationship to contributory social insurance:

a. Individuals and heads of families who are beyond effective working ages. Under existing law any supplementation of their resources from public funds must come in the main from means test public assistance.

b. Individuals and heads of families who had low-money incomes in the year covered by the study, but whose difficulties are probably temporary. Youths who have recently entered gainful employment, risk bearers who have had a bad year, persons whose earnings in the year were reduced temporarily by illness, unemployment, or labor disputes are in this category. It may be fairly assumed that if the coverage of old-age and survivors insurance is extended persons who are in this group will be able to attain and maintain an insured status. Those who have irregular earnings may be penalized somewhat by the use of such devices as average earnings and years of covered employment that are involved in the insurance concepts, but these are matters of detail.

c. Chronically poor individuals and families who are marginal or submarginal. It is extremely doubtful whether they can meet the requirements of an insured status under insurance programs of the American pattern. If the present sharp distinction between the contributory insurance and public assistance is continued, they will have to be provided for, if they are provided for at all, through public assistance. Some of the families in this class, notably those of sub-sistence farmers, share croppers, and other poor tenant farmers are relatively large, and the children may be handi-capped by lack of resources. It is the existence of groups of this type that raise the question as to whether the complete coverage of the New Zealand system financed through a universal, fixed rate income tax is not a superior device in meeting the needs of the chronically poor.

2. The chronically poor, whether their poverty is due to age, other misfortune, or their marginal or submar-ginal status, will derive little advantage from the contribu-tory insurances of the American pattern. They are, how-ever, probably the most needy persons in the country. It is realistic to anticipate that they will follow leaders who advocate the noncontributory pension philosophy. As was noted in the chapter on public assistance, the individual states can go a long distance in embodying that philosophy in their public assistance legislation.

CHAPTER VI

VETERANS' BENEFITS

Among the various security and health programs of the government, there is one which applies exclusively to former members of the military and naval forces, and their dependents.[1] In view of developments in the provision of comparable protections for citizens generally, a large part of this special program is anachronistic—especially in application to veterans of World War II. Nevertheless, there has been no abatement in the tendency of veterans to ask for special treatment. Such demands of course rest primarily on grounds of historical precedent, whereby each group seeks parity with the veterans of preceding wars.

Beginning with the Revolutionary War, the United States has provided special benefits for veterans of each war in which it has engaged and for their survivors. These wars include not only the major conflicts in our history, but also the struggle with the Indians which continued intermittently throughout the last century. They include, along with the Spanish-American War, expeditions to quell the Philippines Insurrection and the Boxer Rebellion. Benefits extend also to veterans of the Regular Establishment, that is, of military service in peacetime. Beneficiaries now include many female citizens, not merely as dependents or survivors of veterans, but as former wearers of the uniform. Indeed, the only veterans who have ever been excluded from some form of care by the nation are those who were not in the service of the United States—such as members of the Confederate armies or volunteers in the service of other countries.

Participation in two world wars has enlarged both the actual and the potential number of individuals to whom

[1] These are provided under auspices of the Veterans' Administration. As constituted in 1930, this agency took over functions formerly administered by the Bureau of Pensions (Department of the Interior), the United States Veterans' Bureau, and the National Home for Disabled Volunteer Soldiers.

veterans' benefits apply. Veterans alone now number 19 millions, or about two-fifths of the adult males in the United States. Together with their families they constitute one third of the total population. Moreover, even if there are no more wars, their proportion will increase. If we maintain a standing army of 1.5 million men and continue the draft, there will be an annual increment of about 400,000 new veterans. Marriages and births will produce an increase in veterans' families to an estimated 62.5 million persons by 1957. Despite intervening growth in total population, they will then constitute about 41 per cent of the total.

The benefits granted specifically to this segment of the population are remarkable for their generosity and diversity. This may be indicated in two ways. First, the aggregate cost of benefits over the years has tended to exceed the direct military costs of the wars to which they relate. Pensions to veterans of the Civil War have amounted to over 8 billion dollars, compared with an estimated military cost of 7 billion dollars (excluding interest on the war debt). The war with Spain was on the scale of a police action, costing 643 million dollars and resulting in few casualties, but its veterans have received nearly 3 billion dollars. The cumulative expenditures for veterans of World War I is already comparable to the military cost of that conflict, which was 24.5 billion dollars.

Second, because of provisions for non-service-connected disabilities, old age, and survivors, the costs continue over a long period of time. International comparisons show that other nations have confined their care of veterans mainly to service gratuities and to individuals who were maimed or disabled in combat; as a result, they have experienced their heaviest expenditures for veterans in the early part of the postwar period. In contrast, after every war the peak of expenditures by the United States has not been reached until 50 to 65 years after the fighting was over. Although our provisions for disabled veterans are more generous than those of other countries (about double the rates afforded by Canada and over four times as large as British allowances), they are only a small part of the program. The end of expenditures for the War of 1812 was reached only three years ago; we are still paying for the war with Mexico; in the case of the War of 1812 the peak occurred in 1880, while in the case of the Civil War it was experienced as recently as 1921. The annual expenditures for veterans of the war with Spain and World War I are still increasing.

A similar trend for veterans of World War II is still in a very early stage. For them, an increasing rate of expenditures over the next three decades is virtually assured by their advancing age. Later on, this trend will be modified by their mortality. Even in the year 2000, however, it is expected that some 3.8 million veterans of World War II will still be living. As this number equals that of the veterans of World War I who are now living, it is apparent that the costs will be at high levels throughout the next half century.

While such figures show the long-range importance of the benefits, estimates of their total cost or of annual costs prevailing 50 years from now have limited value. In the first place, such estimates mean something only in relation to the national income, which may also expand during this period. In the second place, estimates necessitate assumptions with respect to the nature and structure of benefits which will be available to veterans at any given time. It is therefore more practical to center attention on the short-range outlook, which when grouped with other estimated commitments under current law or proposals reveals sufficiently the magnitude of this burden. For the immediate future, the prospect is one of temporary decline, followed after three or four years by a resumption of an upward trend.

In this chapter, the reasons for the trend and its significance for this study will be dealt with in four parts. Certain

benefits which will be of limited importance in the future
will first be considered; although they have constituted a
substantial portion of expenditures since the war, these
items are now diminishing. Second, attention will be
turned to those benefits which, as permanent commitments,
will more than offset trends in the first group. Third, benefits in the latter group will be discussed from the viewpoint
of pyramiding—that is, a functional duplication—of benefits under other security programs. Finally, appraisal of
the situation which is expected to prevail ten years hence
will include a discussion of political pressures which can be
expected to operate, in the ensuing years, to render obsolete
any estimates which can be prepared now.

TEMPORARY BENEFITS

The significant items in this category are the so-called
readjustment benefits, which from now on will taper off and
terminate altogether within ten years, unless legislative
authorizations are amended. These benefits, which were
aimed at the problems of transition from military to civilian
life, include unemployment allowances, subsistence and
tuition for purposes of education, and guaranty of loans.
They also include pensions to the extent that they are increased (temporarily) for the period of training involved
in the rehabilitation of disabled veterans.

Although such benefits have cost some 11 billion dollars
over the past four years and may total more than 20 billions, they are scheduled to expire on cut-off dates fixed by
the Servicemen's Readjustment Act of 1944, as amended,
or by the Vocational Rehabilitation Act of 1943.[2] Thus,
while payments for any period of unemployment have as-
sisted approximately one half of the veterans of World War

2 Public Law 346, 78 Cong. 2 sess., June 22, 1944 (58 Stat. 284). This
legislation was popularly termed "The G. I. Bill of Rights." Public Law 16,
78 Cong. 1 sess., Mar. 24, 1943 (57 Stat. 43), provided an optional training
benefit applicable exclusively to disabled veterans.

II, there can be no payment under existing law for such periods commencing after July 25, 1952. Assistance for education and training, which has been utilized by more than six million veterans, cannot be provided after July 25, 1956. Provisions for the guaranty of loans have aided nearly 1,700,000 veterans to purchase homes, farms, or business property, but no such loans may be guaranteed after July 25, 1957. However, while this will terminate expenditures in the form of interest which the government pays for one year on the portion of loans guaranteed, there will be continuing expenditures as a result of the contingent obligations which the government has assumed in connection with the principal. Though this obligation might become substantial, we will here assume a low ratio of defaults.

Apart from these temporary benefits, such miscellaneous items as prosthetic appliances, seeing-eye dogs, automobiles for veterans with amputations, and homes for paraplegic veterans, have a highly-specialized purpose and are limited to a relatively small number of veterans.[3] Burial allowances are available for any veteran who was discharged under conditions other than dishonorable, but at the current level of 13 million dollars annually are comparatively negligible.

The benefits which are derived by veterans from their life insurance contracts with the government are not germane to this discussion insofar as they are supported by the (voluntary) contributions of the insured, which are administered as trust funds. However, it should not be overlooked that these contracts, which involve nearly 7 million policies with a total face value of 40 billion dollars, are partially subsidized. There are two classes of expenditure which require direct appropriations from Congress; one covering the value of claims resulting from military haz-

---

[3] The automobiles and other conveyances will have cost about 42 million dollars, but eligibility for such grants terminated June 30, 1949. The housing subsidy of $10,000 each for some 1,300 paralyzed veterans should be completed in 1951.

ards, the other administrative expense. The military death claims were naturally heavy at the end of the war. They have cost nearly 4 billion dollars since 1940, but have declined from 1.4 billions at the peak in 1946 to 75 millions in 1949. Although the expense of administering the insurance is now about 40 million dollars annually, it should be susceptible to contraction. Administrative expense is of course entailed by all types of benefit. It depends on the level of activities at any given time, and should move up or down correspondingly.[4]

Veterans also have numerous intangible benefits, such as preferences for civil service employment, homesteads, and naturalization; priorities for materials used in housing, and special tax exemptions. Such benefits, although worth something to the recipient, are not measurable as they do not correspond to any monetary payment.

PERMANENT COMMITMENTS

We here turn to consideration of benefits which, because of their size and duration, are significant for the purpose of this discussion. These fall into two main subdivisions. The first embraces all types of pensions and compensation that are in the form of monetary payments. The second is provision of services in the form of medical and domiciliary care.

Pensions and compensation. The complicated structure of benefits under this broad heading calls for a technical explanation. Compensation, which was originally intended as a substitute for pensions, differs from the latter in its restriction to veterans with disabilities arising from or aggravated by military service, and it is proportionate in amount to the degree of impairment. Payments to sur-

---

4 While this is true in principle, administrative expenses since the war have been disproportionate. Those identified with special programs, such as pensions, insurance, and medical care, have mushroomed more or less proportionately; those not so classified were up from 1.7 millions in 1940 to 146 millions in 1947. They are now receding somewhat.

vivors for service-connected death are also termed compensation. Although not so designated, and provided on a different scale, the retirement pay of reserve officers is similar in character to compensation of enlisted men.

Pensions relate primarily to the fact, as distinguished from the effects, of military service and are provided at a flat rate. This does not necessarily mean that all veterans or their survivors are entitled to pensions. For living veterans of World Wars I and II, pensions are thus far contingent upon disability (total and permanent), but the origin of the disability is not relevant; for survivors of deceased veterans of these wars pensions are contingent upon income from other sources in less than stipulated amounts. However, for veterans of other conflicts, pensions have long since been available when the veteran reached a given age, and to his dependents when he died; payments for non-service-connected death merely involve stipulations as to the age of the children and the marital status of the widow.

Under the restrictions of existing law, expenditures for pensions and compensation are over 21 billion dollars annually, as of the year ending June 30, 1949. This was the largest annual expenditure in history. At this rate, the entire previous expenditure of 23 billion dollars for comparable purposes will be doubled in the next 11 years. However, instead of declining or remaining stationary during that period, the annual rate of expenditures will be increasing fast enough to double cumulative totals in nine years or less. This expectation of accelerated payments is based on several factors, which vary according to the size and the age-composition of each group of veterans as classified by wars.

For obvious reasons, payments for the Mexican, Civil, and Indian wars have passed their peaks; and except for the light which they shed historically on the trend of pensions for any particular war over a long period of time, they may be ignored as having little future significance. Although pensions for the Spanish-American War are now believed to be at their peak, they will continue in sizable proportions for several years; as in the case of previous groups, the decline which might be expected from mortality has been repeatedly postponed and offset by legislative liberalizations which increased the rates, broadened the basis of eligibility, and advanced the marriage date governing participation of widows.[5] The commitment for veterans of peacetime service is fairly stable, with slight increase expected in the future. However, the commitments for World War I and World War II will both show rapid increases—though for different reasons.

For World War I veterans, who now average about 57 years of age, the dominant factor is degenerative disease. The number receiving disability compensation (service-connected) reached a peak in 1941 and will continue to decline by mortality, but pensions for disability not connected with military service are increasing rapidly. At the same time, the mortality of World War I veterans (which will reach a peak about 1970) involves rapid increases in expenditures for their survivors. This particular component of expenditures has been important since 1944, when pensions were authorized for any World War I widow who has not remarried and whose income does not exceed $1,000 for a single person or $2,500 for a widow with dependents.[6] Because of delayed marriages, age disparities between veterans and spouses, and the longevity of females, the peak in payments for deceased veterans is naturally experienced later than is the case for living veterans; but both will be increasing in the next ten years.

[5] The commitment to veterans of the war with Spain is expected to decline from 165 million dollars to about 130 millions in 1958. At that time, only some 2 million dollars will be payable to beneficiaries of earlier wars.

[6] Prior to this legislation, dependents of World War I veterans were not pensionable unless the veteran was receiving compensation for a service-connected disability at the time of his death.

Similar shifts from emphasis on compensation to emphasis on pensions (with or without existing restrictions as to income and disability) will later operate in the case of World War II veterans. Requirements on their behalf *now,* however, are in great part for the purpose of disability compensation. The size of this benefit, which amounts to over one half of the total for this group, is attributable to the sheer weight of numbers involved in the World War II mobilization. Although review procedures have resulted in a moderate reduction of the case load, the expenditures have continued to rise because of increases in the average degree of disability and the average payment per case. The case load would be expanded greatly in event of enactment of statutory presumptions of service-connection for certain types of chronic diseases which are not traceable to military service on the basis of medical evidence. As enacted for World War I veterans in 1923 and 1924, this type of legislation profoundly affected the trend of expenditures for that group.

The next largest component of World War II expenditures is for the account of the deceased veterans of that conflict. Although combat deaths—in ratio to the numbers involved—were less than anticipated, there is a continuing accretion to the load from deaths after discharge from the Army or Navy which, under existing regulations, relate to service. The third largest component of expenditures relates to the retirement of reserve officers. The number of these cases on June 30, 1949 was only 30,399 as compared with 1,638,534 veterans of World War II receiving disability compensation, but the rates of payment per case average about three times as high.[7] Because of

---

[7] This is due to differences in the statutory background. Special legislation has placed temporary officers of the Army of the United States (and World War I emergency officers) on the same basis as regular officers, or three fourths of base pay, when retired for any disability. The amount of compensation to which enlisted men are entitled depends on the degree of impairment involved in the disability.

the comparative youth of World War II veterans, payments for non-service-connected disability are as yet comparatively light, but they will be increasing somewhat in the next 10 years, as a result of the hazards of civilian life.

While the upward trend of benefits, taken as a whole, is unmistakable, the rate and extent of the increase is much more difficult to determine. The difficulty is that the precise magnitude of benefits 10, 20, or 50 years hence is not merely an actuarial problem, though this alone has variable aspects. For example, it is fairly easy to determine, from actuarial projections of the number of veterans by age groups, that obligations to World War I veterans under existing law will reach a peak between 1964 and 1968, and for World War II veterans about the year 1990; and that for both groups combined the peak will be nearer the latter date. Also, it is fairly obvious that declines in expenditures after these dates will either be postponed or flattened out by requirements on behalf of the survivors of deceased veterans in each group. However, the shifting legislative basis cannot be predicted with reasonable accuracy. Therefore, no reliable estimates are available, nor can they be prepared. Official estimates are confined to immediate needs of the Veterans Administration for purposes of annual presentation of the budget; even these are frequently modified by requests for deficiency appropriations which are deemed essential for the fulfillment of obligations or commitments arising in the course of fiscal operations. In fact, these deficiency appropriations for the Veterans Administration have become the rule rather than the exception.

In spite of difficulties, certain estimates have placed the cost of pensions and compensation in 1958 in the neighborhood of 2.7 billion dollars.[8] This total includes 1.6 billions

8 Report of the Trundle Engineering Company on the Veterans' Administration to the Commission on Organization of the Executive Branch of the Government, House Committee Print 14, 81 Cong. 1 sess., p. 64.

for World War II and 956 millions for World War I. Comparison of these figures with current disbursements indicates an increase in the rate of expenditures of approximatey one-half billion dollars for each of the two groups in the next ten years.[9] Despite the smaller number involved, the increase for World War I is equal to that for World War II because the veterans are an older group. The reduction for other groups is expected to be only about 42 millions. However, the estimates cited above do not include the cost of legislation which has been passed since they were prepared. Projections of the cost of new legislation are customarily limited to the first year following enactment, but these indicate that the size of additional commitments would raise the estimate for 1958 to at least 3 billions on the basis of existing laws.[10]

Although projections of cost cannot take into account the uncertainties involved in future legislation, the possibilities should not be ignored. The unit cost (or average payment per case) has been subjected periodically to increases "in line with increases in the cost of living and the increased wages paid by private industries and the government." Apart from legislation affecting unit cost, however, the most important question now pending is the broadening of pension coverage to include all veterans of World War I and World War II on reaching the age of 65, regardless of disability or any test of employability. While proposals of this character have so far failed of enactment, they will gain momentum with the approach of the election campaigns of 1952 and 1956.[11] The total cost of world

[9] Disbursements in 1948 were 1.1 billions and 472 millions, for World War II and World War I respectively. For purposes of comparison, the latter figure excludes extra pensions under Public Law 16, which expire in 1956.

[10] One of two pieces of legislation (Public Law 339, 81 Cong. 1 sess., Oct. 10, 1949), referred to here has become law while this chapter was being written.

[11] H. R. 4617, 81 Cong. 1 sess. which would create such a pension in amount of $72 per month, subject only to income limitations of $1,200 per annum (or $2,500 if married), passed the House on June 1, 1949.

war pensions at age 65 (and supplementary features for those under 65) has been estimated by the Veterans Administration at not less than 65 billion dollars. While the severest impact of this cost in terms of annual expenditures would not be felt until a later date, it would already be expensive in 1960, when half of the 2,630,000 veterans of World War I who will still be living will have passed the age of 65. Since some of them would qualify for a disability benefit under existing law, accurate estimates of the additional cost which would be entailed by old-age pensions necessitate subtractions for those who would merely acquire an option as to the type of benefit which they would receive. Nevertheless, the net addition in 1960 would exceed a billion dollars, with heavier disbursements in prospect later as World War II veterans grow older.

Thus, the potential aggregate of pensions and compensation in 1960 is about 4 billion dollars. After 1964 both the number of World War I veterans living and the number over 65 will be declining. However, the number of World War II veterans over 65 will be increasing from about 37,000 in 1960 to a peak of 6,536,000 in 1990.

Medical care. The medical, hospital, and domiciliary services of the Veterans Administration are less costly than benefits in the form of pensions and compensation. However, they constitute another long-range, increasing commitment. As applicable to World War I veterans, these functions have been expanding until recently. Meanwhile, veterans of World War II have received identical rights.[12]

However, the rights of specific individuals depends on the particular form of care which is required. For conditions which do not require hospitalization, or so-called outpatient treatment, medical care is restricted to veterans

---

[12] Public Law 10, 78 Cong. 1 sess., Mar. 17, 1943 (57 Stat. 21), granted veterans of World War II rights to hospitalization, domiciliary care, and burial benefits on a parity with World War I veterans.

with service-connected disabilities. Care in hospitals is available to all veterans subject to priorities for service-connected disabilities or emergency cases.[13] In principle, the care of non-service-connected disabilities is further limited to veterans who are unable to defray the expense of private hospitalization; the law requires the applicant to affirm under oath that he is financially unable to pay for his own care, but it also provides that his statement shall be accepted as sufficient evidence. Affidavits are not investigated by the Veterans Administration. The organized representatives of veterans are opposed to a means test as stigmatizing them with with a "pauper" status. Widespread abuses involving individuals who can afford private care have been reported. The limitation of hospital care to those actually needing free service thus appears to be more verbal than substantial.

Due to the differences in the basis of eligibility, as between out-patient and in-patient care, there are two distinct trends in the scope of the medical responsibilities to veterans which the government has assumed. Out-patient activity is limited to a maximum of three million veterans who have or may obtain service-connected ratings of impairment. Since it relates to military rather than to civilian hazards, the out-patient load appears to have reached a peak in 1947. Similarly, hospital care is diminishing in cases which are connected with service. Nevertheless, the hospital load is increasing and, on the basis of experience with World War I veterans, is not expected to reach a peak until about 1975. At any given time, however, it is limited by the capacity of the Veterans Administration to handle applicants, except to the extent that this capacity is augmented by contracts with civil, state, and other federal hospitals.

[13] Care in veterans' homes (so-called domiciliary care), as distinct from hospitals, is not strictly a medical function, but the basis of eligibility is the same as for hospitalization, and the need for it is medically determined.

In 1944 and 1945 Congress authorized an extensive construction program consisting of 90 new veterans' hospitals and 9 additions to existing hospitals, to provide 53,574 more beds. Since the average daily patient loads have not increased quite as much or as fast as anticipated, this program has been curtailed by 16,000 beds under executive order. Unless sights are again raised or lowered, the number of beds now expected to be available by 1960 is 139,000. This figure, which allows for abandonment of some existing units of temporary construction, compares with 123,000 which are now available.

For several reasons, these figures do not constitute a satisfactory guide for estimating operating expenditures. The shortage of doctors and nurses causes operating capacity to be less than physical capacity in terms of hospitals and beds. The use of a given capacity is also affected by the rate of turnover. Since World War II, the average length of patient-stay has been reduced substantially, but it is not clear whether this is due to increased efficiency as claimed, or whether it is due to the change in age composition of patients, which is a temporary factor. Apart from these variations, however, the average daily patient load depends on future policy with respect to the care of non-service-connected disabilities. It is significant that the greater part of the current load, even for World War II, relates to such cases. When the future need for hospitalization is projected in terms of all veterans, regardless of the nature of disabilities, the authorized expansion of facilities (with or without the recent cut-back) appears inadequate to accommodate it. At the same time, existing capacity is more than adequate to accommodate the burden resulting from service. Under the circumstances, there can be no intelligent planning of hospital expansion unless Congress redefines the hospitalization commitment.

The other main factor in the level of expenditures is unit cost, or average cost per patient-day. This has varied from an average of $2.78 in 1941 to $9.05 in 1948.[14]   Obviously, this increase pertains to salary levels and fluctuations in the prices of goods and services.   Although predictions are hazardous, we cannot expect costs to decline much from existing levels, particularly as the increased cost of personnel is attributable to reorganization of the Department of Medicine and Surgery (in 1946) under authorization of Congress to permit needed improvement in the quality of medical care.

During the period which intervened between the two world wars, the expenditures of the Veterans Administration in this field ranged from 30 to 60 million dollars per year.   They have now risen to levels approaching 600 million dollars.   These figures do not include expenditures for construction which should be completed well before 1960.[15]   They do, however, cover medical examinations which are auxiliary to the provision of benefits in the form of pensions, insurance, and vocational rehabilitation.   This work is incidental to the maintenance of plant and personnel for purposes of treatment.   The figures also include expenditures for research, prosthetic appliances, physical rehabilitation, and recreation services.

In view of the complexity of functions and the uncertainties described above, the future cost of medical services is peculiarly difficult to estimate.   Figures prepared by a task force for the Hoover Commission have placed the cost of hospitalization and medical care in 1958 at $1,226,000,000 (excluding construction).   This estimate was arrived at on the basis of a bed requirement of 192,000 and operating costs of $8.73 per patient-day.   It was also assumed that the cost of out-patient and other medical work will equal the cost of operating hospitals.

[14] These particular figures represent hospital operation only.   The cost of operating homes is less, but this has increased commensurately.

[15] At the present time roughly one third of the projected new hospitals have been completed, and one third are under construction.   The other third are still in the planning stage.

This estimate seems high. A considerable increase was to be expected as an impact of World War II. However, the three to fourfold increase in veteran population does not explain the tenfold increase of expenditures for medical care which has been experienced. The volume of out-patient activity increased from 1,066,729 treatments in 1940 to 5,220,336 in 1947, but is now diminishing; further, a larger proportion of this may be taken care of in the future by the medical personnel of the Veterans Administration instead of on a fee basis by private physicians. Although the hospital load will undoubtedly increase, it has not gone up as fast as was expected. Measured by the number of patients under the care of the Veterans Administration on June 30, this load has increased from 73,114 in 1940 to 124,804 in 1949, or 58.6 per cent.[16] These figures do not include the backlog of applicants awaiting admission, but neither are these reflected in expenditures. Since the scale of expenditures is ultimately governed by the amount appropriated for the purpose, it is to be hoped that future budgets will be scrutinized with a view to controlling unit costs, if this can be achieved without prejudice to the services which they are intended to provide. Subject to the need for a more exhaustive analysis of this problem than is available from any known source, the estimate of costs ten years hence is placed in the neighborhood of one billion dollars, plus or minus.

VETERANS' BENEFITS AS SOCIAL SECURITY

Much of the special aid to veterans is similar in character to benefits that may also accrue to them under OASI and other programs, although it is provided under differ-

---

[16] The number of veterans in homes has remained nearly stationary—16,267 as compared with 16,518 in 1940. Patients in veterans' hospitals have increased from 52,844 to 96,070. Patients in other hospitals (at expense of the Veterans Administration) have increased from 3,752 to 12,467.

ent laws and administered independently. In addition, as in the case of social security benefits for citizens generally, these benefits are financed solely by the taxing (and borrowing) power of the government, without any corresponding contribution to the national income or the national product.[17] It is therefore doubly desirable to consider the duplicate aspects of protections which are thus provided for many citizens largely without reference to each other.

The similarity is particularly true with respect to the long-term aspects of veterans' relief (discussed in the preceding section), such as provisions for old age, disability, survivors, and medical care. Compensation for war injuries is similar to workmen's compensation for injuries in the course of employment. Pensions for non-service-connected disability or for old age establish guaranteed incomes to veterans merely because of their record of military service, whereas under the philosophy of social security such guarantees embrace all citizens. Pensions to the survivors of deceased veterans are analogous to survivors' benefits under OASI; also the veterans' burial benefit is identical both in kind and amount with that now payable under OASI to insured workers who do not have survivors eligible for money benefits.[18]

These comparisons show the need for reducing the structure of veterans' benefits to a more equitable and reasonable basis. With respect to medical care, the element of duplication relates to proposals for public health insurance, which are impending along with proposals for expansion of OASI. As will be developed in another study by the Brookings Institution, coverage would tend to depend

---

[17] The analogy is consistent with statistical procedures, which classify government expenditures in terms of a distinction between "transfer payments" and "payments for goods and services."

[18] Under pending legislation the burial benefit under OASI would be payable regardless of survivors.

on the availability of medical services, regardless of the means or agencies by which they are provided. With existing limitations on capacity for the provision of such services in terms of the supply of doctors, nurses, and physical plant, some integration of programs under government auspices will almost certainly be forced.

Although integration of pension programs is equally desirable, this is much less certain of achievement due to the monetary character of the benefits and the entrenchment of veterans' claims to the privilege of special treatment. Nevertheless, if it is the purpose of these benefits not to let aging or otherwise incapacitated veterans live in penury, this theory is no longer applicable. It may be reasonable to give veterans a higher standard of living, in consideration of their war service, than they would otherwise be entitled to, but this should not be done on the assumption (which is increasingly fallacious) that they have nothing else on which to live.

As matters stand, a veteran is not entitled to more than one type of pension for his war service; for instance, he could not draw both disability compensation and an old-age pension from the Veterans Administration. However, there is no provision in existing law which would preclude him from receiving OASI benefits, which have no relation to war service. Payments under a program which is characterized as insurance are independent of pensions or other benefits that may be given to the insured. Further, under the provisions of H.R. 6000 for social security expansion, veterans of World War II would receive credit toward old-age and survivors insurance for the duration of their service as though they had been in covered employment at a salary of $160 a month. Although veterans do not now have credit for military service as employment covered by the Social Security Act, except in the special case of World War II veterans who died within three years of separation from the service, this proposal clearly involves pyramiding.[19]

On the other hand, eligibility for certain types of veterans' pensions is subject to limitations as to income from other sources. As computed for the purposes of such limitations, income includes social security benefits only after the worker has received the full amount of his personal contribution, as distinguished from the contributions of his employers. In the case of benefits received by a widow on the basis of her husband's employment, they are considered income as received. However, even in these cases, the income must exceed $1,000 per annum, if the applicant is single, or $2,500 if he is married or has minor children, in order to exclude him from the additional benefit as a veteran or as the survivor of a deceased veteran.[20] Therefor, unless these limits are revised downward or unless social security benefits are increased substantially on the average, existing bars to entitlement under both programs are practically ineffective.

In the majority of cases, it thus appears that beneficiaries of veterans' laws who also acquire an insured status under social security have a duplicate protection for the same hazards.

PRESSURES FOR EXPANSION

Rough estimates have placed the costs that will prevail ten years hence, for veterans' pensions and medical care, in the neighborhood of 4 billion dollars—assuming stabil-

---

[19] Under existing amendments, widows of veterans who died within three years of separation from service may receive social security death benefits, if not in receipt of pension or compensation from the Veterans Administration.

[20] These limitations relate to the payment of pensions to veterans of World War I and World War II for non-service-connected disability; and to pensions for widows and children of deceased veterans of those wars. They do not apply to disability compensation or pensions for service-connected death. For purposes of the proposed age pension to veterans of World Wars I and II, as passed by the House of Representatives June 1, 1949, the limits of income barring eligibility would be $1,200 and $2,500.

ity of existing law, which is unrealistic. These figures are exclusive of types of benefit which are not comparable to social security and of administrative expenses.

They also exclude the possibility of a federal bonus to veterans of World War II, such as World War I veterans received in 1936.[21] The World War I bonus (formally designated as adjusted compensation) was authorized under pressure which culminated in riots and civil disturbances and which prevailed in the face of arguments centering on cost. Due to the greater number of beneficiaries and the duration of their service, the estimated cost of bonuses for World War II veterans ranges in the neighborhood of 30 billion dollars, depending on the terms. There is already considerable discussion of this subject, but veterans' organizations are not yet in agreement on the feasibility or strategy of bonus requests. At this juncture, greater certainty attaches to legislation which is pending in respect to pensions. Taking account of pension proposals which are likely to be approved raises the estimate for pensions and medical care to 5 billion dollars.

This approach is consistent with the historical tendency to liberalize veterans' laws—a history which indicates the remarkable persistence of proposals that do not achieve passage at any one session of Congress. The national legislature registers a high degree of sensitivity to veteran constituents, whose ratio is now vastly increased in all districts. The evidence of this sensitivity lies in the large (frequently unanimous) majorities which are recorded on measures which come to a vote, particularly in the House. Sometimes, the executive branch of the government has exercised a restraining hand, as in bonus legislation, but all vetoes

21 This World War I pattern of bonus payment has already been repeated by the states. Thus far, approximately 2.9 billion dollars worth of bonuses have either been authorized or are awaiting final approval in scheduled referenda and legislative sessions. However, the case for payment by the states has differed from that of the federal government in respect to their financial condition at the end of the war.

of veterans' laws have been overridden, either in the same or subsequent sessions of Congress. While most of the large number of bills relating to veterans' affairs which are introduced in every session are not reported out of committee, the number and variety of those which do become law have resulted in a "confused, overlapping, unrelated crazy-quilt of benefits."

The history of veterans' legislation is one of failure to stabilize benefits in terms of a guiding policy. With each succeeding war, the policy of the United States has first been restricted (as in other countries) to the care of the war-disabled and the survivors of the war dead. In the course of time, this has always been expanded to the care of all veterans and their survivors. During World War I the military pension system was purposely discarded except in application to the veterans of previous wars for the remaining terms of their survival. For the new veterans, benefits were substituted in the form of compensation for service-connected death and disability, vocational rehabilitation, and life insurance. At the same time, medical care (not previously provided) was inaugurated. In the light of subsequent events, however, these benefits were not substitutions; rather, they were added to the pension system.

With the outbreak of World War II, all benefits then available to World War I veterans were increased in amount and extended to participants in the new conflict. In addition, World War II veterans were given readjustment benefits, which were unprecedented except in the sense that they are loosely comparable to the World War I bonus as constituting a recompense for the sacrifices entailed by military service. The substitution was explicit in the Servicemen's Readjustment Act, as originally enacted by the Seventy-eighth Congress, which provided for the deduction of benefits therein authorized from any allowance in the nature of "adjusted compensation" that might later be authorized.[22]

22 Sec. 1505, Title 6.

However, this provision was repealed by the Seventy-ninth Congress because it was considered a deterrent to the use of current benefits by many veterans and an unwarranted binder on future congresses.

Meanwhile, the pension system which was supposedly abandoned in 1917 has been largely reinstated for veterans of both world wars. The first breach in World War I veteran policy occurred in 1930 with authorization of payments which, while contingent on disability, did not require service-connection. This partial lowering of the bars is now giving way to pensions which are not even contingent upon disability. During the recent conflict, pensions also were authorized for widows of World War I veterans, contingent only on income stipulations. This action not only resurrected the policy toward survivors of Civil War veterans, but establishes a powerful precedent for similar provisions on behalf of the widows of World War II veterans.

The force of precedent has been the greatest single factor in shaping the anachronistic course of veterans' legislation. Some of it is justified in economic terms. If history repeats itself, the possibility of new bonus legislation is dependent on future conditions of employment. Adjustments affecting the unit cost of benefits are often related to price levels; since 1939, for example, thirty public laws have been enacted which provide increased rates or liberalize pension or compensation payments to keep pace with the increased cost of living. In this connection, there is an important question whether there should not also be commensurate reductions when there is a decline in the cost of living. However, the main stream of argument is not essentially economic, but one of equity as between the veterans of different wars. As each group of veterans grows older and becomes better organized, it seeks authorization of benefits comparable to those which were available to veterans of wars more remote in history. Just as Spanish-American War veterans have always sought parity with veterans of the Civil War, World

War I veterans seek parity with veterans of the war with Spain. As they grow older, veterans of World War II will just as surely cite benefits to World War I veterans as justification of their case. In fact, they are already on a par insofar as the rights of living veterans are concerned. Existing disparities relate to the survivors of deceased veterans.

Wherever it appears, the case for equity ignores the substitution of benefits which were not available to former groups. Thus, with each succeding war the benefits tend to increase in geometric as well as arithmetic proportions; that is, they are multiplied not only by such factors as the number of veterans and the duration of their service, but by legislative liberalization over the years. This process is, quite simply, a response to political pressure. The irresponsibility of this is particularly striking when a pension lobby argues (as is notable in the case of veterans of the war with Spain) that veterans themselves make up for increased costs by their mortality, which reduces the number eligible under a given framework; in this way, benefits which would otherwise be declining have been expanded.

The underlying philosophy of veterans' benefits is the doctrine that they constitute repayment of a debt owed by the nation. The nature of this debt transcends financial criteria, and there has never been the slightest question of its justice in the case of those who do not return from military service intact. For all others, however, we have gone farther than any other nation and should now face the question of what we can afford in this field. In the case of those whose service was of short duration or who were not exposed to the hazards of warfare, the debt may actually be repaid several times over. This situation applies, for example, to women veterans whose duties did not differ essentially from those of civilian employees of the Army and Navy. Doubtless, a large percentage of male veterans were in a comparable situation. In World War I only about half of the number mobilized were sent overseas, and only about half of those sent overseas saw service at the front. In World War II, a larger number, but not necessarily a larger proportion, served on battle fronts around the world, while a larger number also served in a nonhazardous capacity.

Except in the case of the disabled veteran, when the disablement is the result of service, the claim of veterans to special treatment over and above the claim of ordinary citizens is emotional, often specious, in its nature. While no prediction can be made of the extent to which it will continue to prevail, this claim should be controlled in terms of the cost, not only to the American people as a whole but also to the beneficiaries.

CHAPTER VII

PRIVATE PENSION AND RETIREMENT SYSTEMS

Over the past four decades industrial corporations have increasingly adopted various types of health insurance and welfare programs for their employees. In part because of continuing financial commitments involved, pension systems have been instituted much less extensively. In the 1920's and again during the last few years, increased attention has been given to the problems of retirement. Nearly all of the existing pension plans have been established since Social Security began operations and hence are geared as a supplement to the federal system. Recent developments in the field of labor-management relations considered in conjunction with potential changes in old-age and survivors insurance point to certain problems with respect to private pension systems. The purpose of this chapter is to survey these forces which have developed and to present some issues with which management is likely to be faced in the near future.

GENERAL PROVISIONS

The provisions of pension plans vary widely. The age of retirement ranges from 55 to 70 years of age, and often differs with respect to men and women. There is considerable variation in the amounts of retirement benefits. There are several methods of handling funds which now are usually set aside annually to meet future obligations. In some plans, a trust fund is set up with investment of the fund supervised by company officials, by a bank, or by a trust company. In other cases, the annual payments are used to buy annuities. A number of plans require the employer to pay a certain percentage of the pay roll to an independent fund, managed by a union or by a board representing the union, employers, and the public. Plans differ as to the equity or claim an employee may have in the retirement fund. In a relatively few no rights vest; in some there is a partial vestment; in the majority the right of the employee, after fulfillment of certain minimum conditions, is complete and irrevocable.

There are two principal methods of financing retirement systems. One method involves contributions by both employee and employer; the other is financed entirely by the employer and is referred to as the noncontributory method. In analyzing the impact on pensions resulting from recent and impending developments, we shall be primarily concerned with those plans which are financed solely by the employer, whether they are commonly referred to as company pensions, union pensions, or trust funds administered by a board of trustees representing labor, management, and the public.

UNDERLYING MOTIVES

Retirement programs have been adopted for a variety of considerations. Rewarding long and faithful service has probably been one of the more important motives. In this light, the pension is regarded as deferred compensation. Akin to this justification is the view that a pension program enables a company to fulfill its responsibility to the older workers. Some companies regard the pension as a necessary part of a sound over-all personnel policy that permits management to retire aged workers when they are no longer efficient. Their retirement provides an opportunity to promote younger employees to positions of responsibility. The infusion of new ideas and aggressiveness resulting from the advancement of the more youthful workers is beneficial to the company. In some cases the pension has been used to promote stability in the labor force of the company in the hope that it would reduce turnover. This objective was of considerable significance during the war when the supply of labor was particularly tight.

Another justification for the pension is the view that the aging worker is comparable to the wearing out of plant and equipment and should be provided for in the same manner.[1] A consistent depreciation policy that will take into account the deterioration of physical capital, while at the same time providing all or part of the funds for replacements, has long been considered essential. Similarly, the establishment of a fund which will permit the retirement of the old workers tends to maintain the efficiency of the work force at a high level.[2]

Two developments during the War stimulated the growth of industrial pensions, particularly those financed by the employers. One was changes in the Revenue Act of 1942. The provisions with respect to company contributions to pension funds were clarified. In addition, a procedure was instituted whereby a company could consult with the Bureau of Internal Revenue and receive advance approval for tax purposes of its proposed pension plan. Thus a company was virtually certain that its retirement payments within limits would be recognized as legitimate tax deductions before the plan was put into operation. Of greater significance was the imposition of very high corporate income tax rates and also excess income taxes. Thus the major share of a pension would be financed by funds which would otherwise have been paid to the government in taxes.

The growth in the number of industrial pensions since the passage of this Revenue Act is indicated by data fur-

---

[1] This view with respect to retirement benefits is receiving union acceptance. One labor official has recently stated that the "repair and replacement of [the employer's] 'human machines' is . . . a legitimate responsibility of business" and that a floor of protection is the responsibility of government. See a "Communication" by Harry Becker, Director, Social Security Department, UAW, in *Washington Post*, Oct. 16, 1949. The implication is that workers are merely commodities, and hence no responsibility can be placed on the individual to make any provision for his later years.

[2] National Industrial Conference Board, *Trends in Company Pension Plans*, Studies in Personnel Policy 61 (April 1944), p. 5.

nished by the Bureau of Internal Revenue. In the three years up to June 30, 1945 the Bureau had reviewed and approved about 8,500 plans and is approving new plans at the rate of about 1,000 a year.[3]

The second factor in the growth of company pensions was their use during World War II as a device to circumvent wage control. Price control, it will be recalled, was ineffective until the "hold the line" order in April 1943 forced the War Labor Board to prevent further wage rises. During the ensuing two years (until the lifting of wage control in August 1945), most increases in wages were confined to the so-called "fringe" adjustments. Some companies, however, were allowed to grant pensions in lieu of an increase in wage rates.[4]

A sound pension program should provide benefits to both employees and employer. Workers are chiefly concerned with the permanence of the plan, for it is this factor which gives some measure of security and allays the worry and fears with respect to unemployability and dependency in old age. The company should benefit over the years to the extent that the pension system contributes to the maintenance of an efficient labor force and improves the general morale and labor-management relations. The existence of the pension may also better the relations of the company with the public. It may be observed that realization of the benefits by the company hinges in large part on the advantages of the scheme to the employees.

Continuance of a pension for a long period of years depends upon several factors—the most important of which is the ability of the company to make the necessary contributions in bad years as well as good ones. Companies

---

[3] These data include profit-sharing plans some of which actually are pension arrangements. The number which are strictly profit-sharing schemes represents a small proportion of the total.

[4] Evan Keith Rowe and Abraham Weiss, "Benefit Plans Under Collective Bargaining," *Monthly Labor Review* (September 1948), p. 230.

with past records of relatively stable production and earnings are obviously in a better position to initiate pensions.

SIGNIFICANCE OF PENSION COSTS

Past experience has shown that the establishment of a program of periodic contributions to a fund in advance of anticipated retirements gives greater protection to a pension system. The onset of the depression in the 1930's forced many a company to terminate its unfunded pensions because the required expenditures on behalf of retired former employees proved too great a burden.[5] The majority of plans now provide for an annual contribution in anticipation of future pension commitments. These outlays may be pooled in a trusteed fund or used to purchase annuities. In this manner, payment of vested pension rights are assured in future years regardless of the level of business and earnings prevailing at that time.

Management has been well aware of the continuing burden of costs as well as the long-run advantages which may be realized from a soundly conceived pension system. With a view to adjusting the retirement program to fundamental changes in financial conditions, competitive position, or some external factors in the uncertain future, companies tended during the war to adopt plans which were financed by the employer. Although the high tax rates may have been a contributing factor toward this trend, the major consideration was probably the desir-

[5] Recently the United Mine Workers Welfare and Retirement Fund, a pay-as-you-go system, was forced to discontinue pensions to about 20,000 retired miners. This suspension has occurred little more than a year after the initiation of the program and long before the full load of pensions had been assumed. The immediate cause was the cessation of work by the miners and of payments into the Fund by the coal operators. In this instance, the underlying factor was the lack of a contract rendering any further payments into the fund a misdemeanor under the Taft-Hartley law. The ability of the fund to pay pensions will, however, be similarly restricted during a recession or depression. The security for retired miners rests solely on continued production at a high level.

ability of retaining management control over this significant fraction of total labor costs.[6] The importance of this cost element is indicated in a recent study of company pension plans. The investigation found several new plans which provided for employee contributions in years when the companies were unable to make the required outlays of funds.[7] Since the war, more than half of the new and revised pension plans have involved contributions of employees.[8] In view of the sharp increase in wage rates since the abandonment of wage control in the autumn of 1945, management has apparently decided that the outlays for pensions can be better kept within reasonable bounds if the employee bears part of the cost.

The cost increases which resulted from the passage of the Social Security Act of 1935 caused many companies to adjust their own pension benefits downward, in an effort to hold down their costs. This process was repeated with the amendments of 1939. Today many of the larger pension programs are integrated with OASI. One type of plan provides for company retirement payments only to those with wages or salaries above $3,000—the top limit of wage coverage under OASI. Another type offers a minimum pension of a stated amount with a deduction equal to half of the old-age retirement benefit which the pensioner receives from the federal system. Other methods are employed but the purpose—common to all—is to avoid unnecessary costs. Without this adjustment in a pension program, a company would be paying taxes on its pay roll for covered wages and salaries and making duplicating

6 Decisions of the War Labor Board granting "fringe" wage increases in the form of company-financed pensions comprised another factor contributing to this trend.

7 National Industrial Conference Board, *Trends in Company Pension Plans*, p. 18.

8 The National Industrial Conference Board has recently released a study of 255 pension plans adopted since October 1945. The authors found that 58.8 per cent of these involved a contribution by both employee and employer. See *Management Record* (October 1949), p. 428.

outlays for the company pension on all wages and salaries in the pay range up to $3,000.

With any change in salary coverage under OASI, such as is proposed in H.R. 2893 or H.R. 6000, probably most companies would shortly re-examine their plans with the view to holding down total pension costs by integrating at the higher "covered" salary level. This review and adjustment will be in order with every change in the future, and upward revisions of OASI may be expected with changes in the cost of living, minimum standards of living, and with new conceptions of what the country can afford.

PENSIONS AND COLLECTIVE BARGAINING

Management no longer has freedom of action and decision with respect to company pensions. In the past, employers have usually made changes in their pension systems without consulting or bargaining. In many cases the non-contributory trust fund type of plan has been selected chiefly because it gives management maximum control over pension policies. In a recent case before the National Labor Relations Board, the decision of the Board was that the Inland Steel Company could not change the provisions of the pension system without bargaining with the employees. The pension was held to constitute deferred compensation and thus must be regarded as a part of wages and subject to collective bargaining. The Seventh Circuit Court of Appeals upheld this decision, and the Supreme Court has refused to review the case.[9] With the exception of those industrial concerns which are not dealing with strongly organized unions, effective control of pension policy and of pension costs has been taken away from management.

Employers now have to recognize that the establishment and revision of pension plans are within the scope of collective bargaining and are part of compensation for services. Thus the unions may seek higher immediate wages, more

---

[9] See 77 NLRB 1; 7th Circuit Court, 170 Fed. (2d) 247; 336 U. S. 960.

favorable pension provisions or both. The evidence suggests that individual workers, whether in white collar or in overalls, are not concerned with the insecurity of old age until they are 40 or 45 years old. The younger workers are more interested in getting wage increases as take home pay, and most company labor forces are youthful in terms of average age. For example, in 1947 when the workers of the Ford Company were given the choice of an immediate fifteen cent an hour wage increase as take home pay or the equivalent represented by a retirement plan and only a seven cent an hour increase in pay, the rank and file union members voted overwhelmingly for the entire increase as take home pay.[10]

Union leaders are in a different position. They must maintain their personal prestige and strengthen the union. As past experience has indicated, if for any reason demands for increased pay cannot be successfully pressed at the moment, a demand for pensions presents an alternative. If one labor leader succeeds in getting pensions for his union, other leaders must seek to equal his achievements. Thus it seems probable that, in the future, demands for pension systems and their revision will be important issues in collective bargaining.

Pension systems established through collective bargaining often operate to tie the employee tightly and permanently to the union. To be eligible for a pension, he must maintain his union membership during both his working years and his retirement. Withdrawal from the union involves forfeiture of pension privileges. The fact that an employee worked under the system for a number of years gives him no contractual or vested right to old-age benefits with respect to those years. The United Mine Workers of America Welfare and Retirement Fund and the National Electrical Benefit Board, for example, specifically provide that the individual worker acquires no con-

---

[10] *New York Times*, Sept. 25, 1947.

tractual or vested interest in a prospective retirement benefit. These discretionary pensions thus may play a major role in the maintenance of union membership—a matter of great concern to labor leaders.

The adjustment of existing noncontributory company pension plans to the governmental system of old-age and survivors insurance is complicated by the court decision that these plans are part of compensation and hence subject to collective bargaining. If an employer on being required to pay additional pay-roll taxes for OASI proposes to reduce his contributions to his own company pension plan, he may and probably will be met in collective bargaining by the argument that such action is a reduction in compensation. This view has already been expressed by a representative of the Eastern Seaboard Alliance of Telephone Unions, an association of eight unions of telephone workers.[11] The fact that some of these plans were established prior to the Social Security Act or prior to amendments expanding old-age and survivors insurance benefits and increasing their cost, apparently does not give the employer the right to abandon his system, although that right was reserved when the system was inaugurated.

MAJOR ISSUES

These recent trends in the private pension field give rise to several vital issues which will here be summarized, although no attempt will be made to suggest or recommend solutions.

1. How are the private pension plans to be tied into the government system of old-age and survivors insurance? If the government should adopt the proposals of the Administration, as contained in H.R. 2893, for an almost universal compulsory retirement system, taxing and basing

11 See *Social Security Act Amendments of 1949,* Hearings before the House Committee on Ways and Means, 81 Cong. 1 sess., Pt. 2, pp. 1803-13.

benefits on earnings up to $4,800, should company pension plans be completely abandoned or should they be continued only as supplementary devices with the OASI benefits deducted from the benefits they offer? Or should the government system pay benefits only to the extent required to insure against want, with the expectation that for many workers they will be supplemented by private devices, among the most important of which are private retirement systems?

2. Private retirement systems have often been adopted to increase the incentives which the particular organization offers its employees. The benefits are part of the compensation for services rendered and are designed to be attractive to the type of workers the organization employs. If the government substitutes a uniform national system alike for all up to the first $4,800 of their earnings, what will be the effect on incentives within the particular organizations where production takes place?

3. Mature retirement systems involve very heavy annual benefit payments. Can the economy afford both a compulsory, almost universal, retirement system such as proposed by H.R. 2893 and private company pension plans? As the taxes to support the government system increase, will the burden of two systems become unbearable? The money to support noncontributory systems set up by management must in the long run come either from profits or from the sale of goods or services. If it comes from profits, it will, under existing tax laws, reduce the amount which the companies would otherwise pay into the federal treasury for general purposes. If the costs become embedded in costs of production, prices will be affected, and the expected benefits from the system would be accordingly reduced.

Issues such as these should be carefully considered before the nation embarks upon a comprehensive plan such as is embodied in H.R. 2893.

PART III

ANALYSIS OF THE OVER-ALL SECURITY PROGRAM

Preceding pages have laid the foundation for the four closely related chapters that constitute Part III. The first of the chapters summarizes the benefits and costs of the various programs previously discussed and gives estimates of over-all costs for the proposed system as a whole. In the second, the problems of financing these social security costs are analyzed. The third chapter considers the costs of government as a whole and the capacity of the nation to carry the load of social security and the other activities of government. The final chapter restates the major financial issues and makes recommendations for the revision of the American system.

CHAPTER VIII

SUMMARY OF BENEFITS AND COSTS

Preceding chapters in the main have dealt with specific programs and the major factors that will determine their costs. In the first part of this chapter, emphasis will be placed on benefits rather than on programs whenever that distinction is significant from the standpoint of costs. The second part of the chapter will present and briefly discuss a table, bringing together the prospective costs of programs that are within the social security field.

If legislators in deciding upon the nature and extent of social security programs give adequate consideration to costs and financing, they will be much concerned not only with the magnitude of costs but also with the question: How quickly will the commitments we make reach maturity and be reflected in full in annual budget statements? How far shall we be committing future generations to a policy the cost of which is largely unpredictable and which might be financially practicable only if domestic and foreign developments are such that the United States can continue the upward climb in economic efficiency that has characterized its previous history?

Another and to some extent related question is how far the legislators should go in writing into the social security laws adopted at this time devices that would operate over the years to effect a redistribution of the earnings of the people to transfer purchasing power from one economic class to another. In social security legislation, redistribution is a consequence of the benefit provisions which determine costs combined with the methods used to raise the money to pay those costs. This chapter will be concerned only with factors affecting redistribution in benefit provisions.

MAJOR BENEFITS

The order in which the several benefits or groups of related benefits will be taken up will be based mainly on the period which must elapse before their costs reach a stable annual level.

Public assistance. Allowances under public assistance can be treated together because the cost load is immediately affected by legislative and administrative action. Liberalization in legal provisions or administration will almost at once result in increased costs, accompanied by budget estimates for increased appropriations. Public assistance is of necessity a transfer of purchasing power from those subject to the taxes used to collect the money to those who do not have enough to live on according to the standard established by legislative and administrative action. The amount of the transfer is, however, limited to that necessary to lift the recipients to the prescribed level. As discussed in the chapter on public assistance, the individual state under the present system determines in large measure the amount to be spent. The system also involves transfers from one state to another through the device of federal grants-in-aid.

In 1948 expenditures for public assistance, national, state, and local, were over 2 billion dollars.[1] Substantial increases within the next few years are to be anticipated. H. R. 6000 provides federal aid for the totally and permanently disabled and increases the part which the national government will contribute for allowances to individuals in all the federal aid categories. Under the open-end grant system, increased federal particpation may further encourage the states to liberalize eligibility requirements and to direct or divert more state funds to federally aided public assistance categories in order to bring federal funds into the state. So far as the states are concerned the system offers liberal grants at low cost and encourages the development of the pension philosophy.

It is commonly asserted that the cost of public assistance will diminish as the insurance programs, especially old-

---

[1] At the time of writing the precise figure for the entire calendar year was not available.

age and survivors insurance, are extended and mature. Classes of persons now provided for under public assistance will be absorbed into the more costly insurance programs. Savings in public assistance will then to a small degree offset the mounting costs of insurance. In the rural states, however, the cost of public assistance programs will continue to increase until and unless subsistence and tenant farmers, agricultural laborers, and other economically weak classes are brought within the contributory insurance system and demonstrate ability to attain and maintain an insured status. A question must be raised as to whether such extension can be made rapidly enough to curb expansion of public assistance in accordance with the pension philosophy.

Compulsory health insurance. The cost of personal medical care as supplied through a national system of compulsory health insurance should fairly promptly reach something approaching a stable load or a gradually increasing load if legislation and administration remain reasonably stable. The time required will depend in part upon the provisions with respect to attaining an insured status. When most of the persons covered have attained that status, the load for temporary illnesses and accidents ought not to vary much from year to year, except when epidemics are experienced. The factors affecting variation in temporary cases would be the growth of the population and health conditions in the particular year. The load for chronic and permanent illnesses and impairments will, however, gradually cumulate over the years.[2]

Under the theory of compulsory health insurance the services available should be alike for all regardless of earnings or income. For reasons which appear insurmountable, persons living in the vicinity of highly developed

---

[2] The law might, however, be so drafted as immediately to extend free personal medical services to persons already retired. If it should, the system would at once assume full load for chronic illnesses and impairment.

medical centers, that is in large centers of population, will get promptly a quality of service which cannot always be made available immediately to dwellers in rural areas upon the happening of an accident or the discovery of an illness. Provision will obviously have to be made for transferring patients from the more remote places to centers equipped to care for the more serious or more obscure difficulties. On the other hand, increases in cost will probably be relatively greater in rural areas than in centers of population because the small numbers served will diminish operating efficiency.

The immediate cost of compulsory health insurance is estimated by Dr. I. S. Falk of the Federal Security Agency as 4.7 billion dollars, increasing to 6.3 billions as the system passes the installation period. The latter figure results in an annual per-capita cost of $50.47.[3] Applying $50 per capita per year to 85 per cent of the future population estimates used by the actuaries of the Social Security Administration would give the following figures, in billions of dollars.[4]

	Based on High Population Estimates	Based on Low Population Estimates
1950	6.2	6.2
1955	6.5	6.4
1960	6.8	6.6
1970	7.1	6.9
1980	7.6	7.2
1990	8.0	7.3
2000	8.5	7.4

These figures, it is believed, can safely be regarded as minimum costs. Unless the experience of the United States

[3] *Social Security Bulletin* (August 1949), pp. 6-7.

[4] Based on Robert J. Myers and E. A. Rasor, *Long-Range Cost Estimates for Expanded Coverage and Liberalized Benefits Proposed to the Old-Age and Survivors Insurance System by H. R. 2893*, Social Security Administration Actuarial Study 28 (February 1949), p. 5. Hereafter cited as Social Security Administration, Actuarial Study 28.

is different from that of England and New Zealand, actual costs will be far higher than the original official estimates.

Dr. Elizabeth W. Wilson, an actuary who has made intensive studies of the cost of compulsory health insurance, arrives at a figure for 1960 about twice that presented by Dr. Falk, or roughly $100 per capita as contrasted with $50. One of the major explanations of the difference is that Dr. Wilson assumes that once compulsory health insurance is introduced pressures will develop for greatly extended services and for almost universal coverage. The United States, according to her assumptions, will move rapidly to the comprehensive services of the English system. Dr. Falk in his article does not project his estimates beyond the year in which the present comparatively limited proposals become fully operative, and hence he makes no allowances for subsequent expansion of services.[5]

Temporary disability. Temporary disability insurance should promptly reach a reasonably stable load if it is strictly administered. It would compensate employed persons, and possibly their dependents, for part of the loss of earnings due to illness or accident. The compensation would be payable for not more than a fixed maximum period. If the disability should last beyond that period, the individual would exhaust his benefit rights and have to be cared for under some other program—permanent disability if he is insured or public assistance if he is not insured and is in need.

Dr. Arthur Altmeyer, Commissioner of Social Security, estimates the cost of temporary disability insurance at 1 per cent of the covered pay roll. One per cent of the estimated current pay roll as used by the actuaries in figuring the costs of H. R. 2893 would yield the following

[5] Dr. Wilson's latest estimates readjusted for increases in price levels are published in the *Christian Science Monitor*, May 17, 1949.

costs, in billions of dollars, for temporary disability insurance.[6]

	Low-Cost Estimates	High-Cost Estimates
1960	1.45	1.46
1970	1.56	1.57
1980	1.65	1.62
1990	1.75	1.66
2000	1.87	1.66

Provisions for temporary disability allowances are not included in H. R. 6000.

The costs of temporary disability insurance will probably increase in periods of recession even under strict administration. Many men—and a smaller proportion of working women—frequently report for duty even if their conditions are such that they could sustain a claim for temporary disability compensation should they remain away from work. The difference between earnings and insurance compensation may be one factor but probably much more important are the attitude toward work and the sense of personal responsibility. Employees may know or like to believe that their presence on the job affects production. If things are slow and dull in the enterprise, the incentive may increase to stay away in event of minor accidents or illnesses or chronic ailments that do not necessarily confine to the home. Unless administration is strict, some employees will take advantage of the system, especially if the difference between actual take-home pay and benefits is not substantial.

Proposals for temporary disability insurance involve redistribution of purchasing power within the system itself. Legislators will determine what percentage of past earnings will be paid as compensation. The percentage will be highest for those with the lowest earnings that will give an

6 Social Security Administration, Actuarial Study 28, p. 10.

insured status. The percentage will diminish as earnings increase; and there will be a maximum beyond which compensation will not go regardless of the earnings of the insured in the base period.

Veterans' benefits. In the chapter on veterans' benefits the fact was stressed that the further cost of those benefits that are comparatively permanent and overlap social insurance will depend on what the Congress does. That matter will not be here summarized or discussed. What needs to be emphasized here is that in the main the veterans are a closed group. Their ages at any time are determined in no small measure by the years during which the United States was at war. As the veterans grow older, the costs of benefits or pensions for them and their dependents will increase through natural forces. The incidence of temporary and permanent disability is generally greater as age advances. Increasing mortality with increasing age means more widows and possibly more other dependents. In this connection the point should be stressed that veterans and their dependents now constitute approximately one third of the population of the United States and that from the standpoint of costs proper co-ordination between veterans' benefits and the social insurances is a matter of profound importance.

Insofar as veterans' benefits are paid only to those who are in need or have earnings or income below a figure fixed by law, an element of redistribution is inherent in the system itself. On the other hand, if all veterans and their dependents are given like benefits under like circumstances, regardless of their economic situation, redistribution is primarily through taxes. Except for premiums on voluntary insurance the veterans as veterans pay nothing directly or specifically for their benefits, although as general taxpayers they may pay heavily, especially if they are financially successful.

For the purpose of indicating in a rough way the magnitude of veterans' benefit payments, the following estimates are presented, in billions of dollars:

1960	5
1970	6
1980	7 to 10
2000	6 to 8

Permanent disability. If benefits to replace part of earnings lost through permanent disability are provided under a no-means test insurance system, costs will increase year by year for many years. Each succeeding year will witness an addition to the number already drawing those benefits, and the number who die in the year will not for many years equal the accessions. Permanent disability insurance has many close resemblances to old-age insurance with respect to the upward movement of costs. The most important difference is that old-age benefits are not payable until the insured attains the age fixed by statute and retires, whereas permanent disability benefits are paid at any time prior to the attainment of that age provided the worker has an insured status. A belief is prevalent that persons retired because of permanent disability are necessarily short-lived, but the fact is that a substantial number of permanently disabling accidents and diseases do not radically affect the expectation of life. Some persons permanently disabled live beyond the normal expectancy of those not disabled. Old-age insurance, moreover, affords almost no opportunity for malingering or fraud beyond the possibility that the applicant or some other interested party can successfully overstate age. Disability insurance does offer some possibilities of malingering and is much more difficult and expensive to administer.

The proposals advanced for permanent disability insurance in H. R. 2893 contain substantially the same arrangements for redistribution of earnings that are inherent in old-age insurance. They will be taken up under that benefit.

Actuarial Study 28 of the Social Security Administration presents the following estimates of cost for the permanent disability provisions of H. R. 2893. They include the cost of supplementary benefits for wives and children. The figures are in millions of dollars.[7]

Year	Low-Cost Estimate	High-Cost Estimate
1960	430	1,148
1970	663	1,564
1980	766	1,762
1990	819	1,832
2000	912	1,961

The great uncertainties regarding the cost of such a program are indicated by the large differences between the low-cost and the high-cost estimates. In every year shown the high-cost estimate is more than double the low-cost.

H. R. 6000 which passed the House as reported by the Ways and Means Committee drastically curtails the provisions with respect to disability. The preliminary data presented in the report of the Committee give a single figure, not the more significant range between a high and a low

COST OF PERMANENT DISABILITY INSURANCE UNDER H. R. 6000 [a]

Calendar Year	Cost as Percentage of Pay Roll		Percentage of Cost Due to Disability	Cost in Millions of Dollars	
	All Programs	Dis-ability		All Programs	Dis-ability
1950	1.1	—	—	1,300	—
1955	2.2	0.2	9.1	2,600	237
1960	3.2	0.4	12.5	3,800	475
1970	4.8	0.6	12.5	6,200	775
1980	6.2	0.6	9.7	8,400	815
1990	7.6	0.6	7.9	10,600	837
2000	8.1	0.6	7.4	11,700	866
Level-premium at 2 per cent interest	6.2	0.5	8.1	—	—

[a] Based on *Social Security Act Amendments of 1949*, H. Rept. 1300, 81 Cong. 1 sess., pp. 34, 35. The minority report gives costs for the disability provisions that are substantially higher. The same, p. 165.

[7] P. 16.

estimate.[8] The table on page 142 is derived from its figures.
On top of these factors is the gradual aging of the population.

Old-age benefits. The phenomenon of annually mounting
benefit costs is most clearly evident and of greatest practical significance in old-age insurance. Starting with no beneficiaries at the outset, the number increases each year as
successive classes pass from the active roll to join those
already on benefit. It is years before the system reaches
full load and the age distribution becomes such that with
full quota at the highest ages the number of deaths in a
year approximately equals accessions. Under a system
that increases benefits according to length of service, each
succeeding class passing to the benefit rolls will for many
years have a higher average benefit than its predecessor.

The old-age insurance benefit proposals involve a substantial measure of redistribution of purchasing power.
H. R. 2893 would subject to taxation and count in determining the amount of benefit all covered earnings not in excess
of $4,800 a year. The benefit formula is so designed that
broadly speaking the ratio of benefits to average earnings
for the best five consecutive years of coverage decreases as
earnings increase. It is highest for those insured whose
earnings are so small that the minimum benefit provisions
are operative, and lowest for those whose earnings are
$4,800 or over. Emphasis should be placed on the fact that
this statement applies to the ratio between benefits and
earnings and not to the absolute amount of benefit. Except
for the minimum provisions, the absolute amount of benefit
goes up with increases in average earnings, but it does not
go up proportionately.

The benefit formula in H.R. 2893 relates the amount of
money given to the insured retired worker to the average
earnings enjoyed by him in his best five consecutive years

---

[8] *Social Security Act Amendments of 1949,* H. Rept. 1300, 81 Cong. 1 sess.

up to but not in excess of $4,800. In other words, it is insuring his money income, although by a percentage that diminishes as his money earnings increase. It is a radically different philosophy from that which underlies many systems in other countries. They seek to assure only a flat uniform benefit that will remove the fear of want. If the insured desires to have in his retirement a larger proportion of his former earnings than the flat benefit will give, he is expected to provide for it himself or get it through the retirement system of the employer or employers for whom he works.

The table presented below shows the estimated cost of the old-age benefits as provided under H.R. 2893. It classifies as old-age benefits those for the worker himself and for wives and widows at or above the retirement age.

COSTS OF OLD-AGE BENEFITS UNDER H. R. 2893[a]
(In millions of dollars)
I. LOW-COST ESTIMATE [b]

| Calendar Year | Total | Old-Age Benefits Under H. R. 2893 | | | |
		Primary	Wife's [c]	Widow's [c]	Parents
1960	3,284	1,849	396	973	66
1970	5,703	3,158	579	1,891	75
1980	7,974	4,608	693	2,597	76
1990	9,868	6,110	735	2,952	71
2000	10,729	6,992	704	2,972	61

II. HIGH-COST ESTIMATE [b]

1960	5,224	3,519	640	949	116
1970	8,528	5,719	916	1,742	151
1980	12,113	8,353	1,212	2,384	164
1990	15,625	11,340	1,433	2,693	159
2000	17,836	13,460	1,520	2,703	153

[a] Based on Social Security Administration, Actuarial Study 28, p. 16.

[b] Based on high employment assumptions and level wage assumption used as actuarial technique for showing relative cost under increasing wage assumption combined with assumption of plan being continually modified to meet such changed conditions.

[c] Includes small amounts for disabled husbands.

H.R. 6000 is much less extreme than H.R. 2893. It uses $3,600 instead of $4,800 as the basis for benefits, employs the average throughout covered service instead of the average for the best five consecutive years and allows a length of service increment of one half of 1 per cent instead of 1 per cent as in the present law and H.R. 2893.

The costs of the old-age benefits of H.R. 6000 are given in the table below.

COSTS OF OLD-AGE BENEFITS UNDER H. R. 6000 [a]

Calendar Year	Costs as Percentage of Pay Roll					Percentage Old-Age Costs to Total Cost	Old-Age Benefits in Millions of Dollars
	All [b]	Primary	Wife's	Widow's	Parents		
1950	0.8	0.6	0.1	0.1	[e]	72.7	945
1955	1.5	1.0	0.2	0.3	[e]	68.2	1,773
1960	2.3	1.5	0.3	0.5	[e]	71.9	2,732
1970	3.7	2.4	0.4	0.9	[e]	77.1	4,780
1980	5.0	3.5	0.4	1.1	[e]	80.6	6,770
1990	6.4	4.7	0.5	1.2	[e]	84.2	8,925
2000	7.0	5.3	0.5	1.2	[e]	86.4	10,109
Level-Premium at 2 per cent interest	5.1	3.7	0.4	1.0	[e]	82.3	

[a] Based on *Social Security Act Amendments of* 1949, H. Rept. 1300, 81 Cong. 1 sess., p. 35.

[b] Does not include lump sum.

[e] Less than 0.05 per cent.

Children's and mothers' benefits. Benefits for children and mothers are of major importance from the standpoint of costs in connection with old-age and permanent disability insurance. Children and mothers may, however, be provided for in unemployment compensation, temporary disability insurance, and medical care. In these three types of insurance the costs for them will emerge fairly promptly. Under old-age insurance, benefits for mothers with dependent children under 18 will increase as the system matures, but they may reach a maximum sooner than old-age benefits will. Primary beneficiaries of advanced age are not likely to leave children under 18 or a widow under 60 who is eligible because she has the care of them. Chil-

COSTS OF BENEFITS FOR CHILDREN AND MOTHERS UNDER H. R. 2893 [a]

Calendar Year	Children		Mothers	
	Low Estimate	High Estimate	Low Estimate	High Estimate
1960	604	473	193	191
1970	744	461	232	192
1980	831	425	257	182
1990	911	391	278	172
2000	985	351	303	166

[a]Data from Social Security Administration, Actuarial Study 28, p. 16. The low and the high relate to the cost of the system as a whole. Conditions which result in low total costs produce relatively high costs for mothers' and children's benefits and vice versa. The more workers who survive to draw old-age benefits, the fewer will leave young widows and children under 18 to draw the benefits provided for these classes.

COSTS OF BENEFITS FOR CHILDREN AND MOTHERS UNDER H. R. 6000 [a]

Calendar Year	Cost as Percentage of Pay Roll			Percentage these Benefits Are of Total Cost	Cost in Millions of Dollars
	Total	Children under 18	Mothers		
1950	0.2	0.2	[b]	18.2	237
1955	0.5	0.4	0.1	22.7	590
1960	0.5	0.4	0.1	15.6	593
1970	0.5	0.4	0.1	10.4	645
1980	0.5	0.4	0.1	8.1	680
1990	0.5	0.4	0.1	6.6	700
2000	0.4	0.3	0.1	4.9	573
Level-premium at 2 per cent interest	0.5	0.4	0.1	8.1	—

[a] Based on *Social Security Act Amendments of* 1949, H. Rept. 1300, 81 Cong. 1 sess., p. 35.

[b] Less than 0.05 per cent.

dren, moreover, lose their eligibility when they attain the age of 18—unless impaired, under the proposed law—and hence this load is not cumulative as is the case with elderly people and the totally disabled.

The costs for mothers' and children's benefits under H.R. 2893 are shown in the table on page 146.

The estimated cost of benefits for children and mothers as provided in H.R. 6000 are shown in the table on page 146.

Unemployment compensation. The dominant factor in determining the long-run cost of unemployment compensation is the unpredictable volume of compensable unemployment. At any given level of total unemployment, the costs will depend mainly on such factors as the extent of coverage, the number who have worked long enough in the base period to attain an insured status, the length of the waiting period, the amount and the duration of benefits, the rules governing disqualifications and penalties, and the efficiency and strictness of administration. As discussed in Chapter II, the American practice has been empirical, to fix a maximum tax and adjust the variables within what it is assumed by the legislature such a tax will support over the years, but with power to reduce the tax through some form of experience rating.

American practice carries a substantial element of redistribution into the benefit formula for compensation. The typical law provides a minimum and a maximum. Between the two the amount and often the duration of benefit turn on the earnings in the period used for determination. Until the maximum is reached, benefits rise with increased earnings. The low-earning employees receive a larger percentage of their earnings as compensation than do those with covered earnings equal to or above the maximum.

Here again American practice insures to a limited degree customary earnings. It does not give to all a uniform flat benefit, varied perhaps solely in accordance with the number dependent on the breadwinner. Under American systems upper bracket employees get more than lower bracket ones but not proportionately more. Except in states which have introduced benefits for dependents, upper bracket single workers with no dependents may receive substantially more than a lower bracket married man with several dependent children who require their mother's care and supervision.

This summary shows that in the big programs of old-age, disability, and survivors insurance and unemployment compensation the United States has gone further than to put a floor of protection under its workers to guarantee them minimum requirements in event of the happening of the contingency. It has put an inclined plane under them. The low end under the workers with lowest counted earnings should in theory give minimum essential protection. The high end gives the workers with maximum covered earnings more protection in actual dollars but less as a percentage of their customary earnings. The proper height for the low end of the plane under the lower bracket employees is susceptible of fairly objective determination. The degree of slope upward from the low point, indeed whether there should be any upward slope at all, is a matter of legislative or political policy.

TOTAL COSTS

In the preceding section of this chapter, the discussion and the presentation of cost figures have been by benefits or groups of benefits. A natural question is, what do the costs amount to in the aggregate? To answer this question a table is presented on page 149 which gives low-cost and high-cost estimates by programs for the five decades 1960 to 2000.

For H.R. 2893, exclusive of temporary disability, the high and the low figures are taken from Actuarial Study 28 of

ESTIMATED AGGREGATE COST OF MAJOR SOCIAL SECURITY PROGRAMS
AND VETERANS' BENEFITS 1960-2000
(In billions of dollars)

I. LOW-COST ESTIMATES

Program	1960	1970	1980	1990	2000
All benefits under H.R. 2893 except					
Temporary Disability	4.65	7.54	10.07	12.15	13.24
Temporary Disability	1.45	1.56	1.65	1.75	1.87
Compulsory Health Insurance	6.60	6.90	7.20	7.30	7.40
Unemployment Compensation	2.95	3.12	3.30	3.50	3.74
Total major insurance programs	15.65	19.12	22.22	24.70	26.25
Public assistance	.90	.80	.70	.60	.50
Veterans' benefits	5.00	6.00	7.00	6.00	6.00
Total low cost	21.55	25.92	29.92	31.30	32.75

II. HIGH-COST ESTIMATES

Program	1960	1970	1980	1990	2000
All benefits under H.R. 2893 except					
Temporary Disability	7.16	10.91	14.69	18.27	20.60
Temporary Disability	2.18	2.34	2.48	2.63	2.81
Compulsory Health Insurance	15.50	16.30	17.00	17.20	17.30
Unemployment Compensation	4.43	4.68	4.95	5.25	5.64
Total major insurance programs	29.27	34.23	39.12	43.35	46.35
Public assistance	1.50	1.20	1.00	.80	.60
Veterans' benefits	5.00	6.00	10.00	9.00	8.00
Total high cost	35.77	41.43	50.12	53.15	54.95

the Social Security Administration. Question has been raised as to whether the assumptions used in this study do not result in an understatement of the possible high costs. The continued maintenance of high levels of employment is assumed. If for any reason the levels of employment should fall below the assumptions, the costs of the system would increase, because more persons would retire on benefits and at earlier and more expensive ages. Despite this possibility the high figures used in the table are taken from Actuarial Study 28. It seems better to use them than to attempt to make original forecasts of the levels of employment that may prevail in the later years of the present century. The figures of aggregate future costs that result from the use of the official estimates are high enough to give a rough idea of the general magnitude of the financial program.

The low figures for the temporary disability provisions of H.R. 2893 are based on Dr. Arthur Altmeyer's statement that this feature would cost 1 per cent of covered pay roll. The high figure assumes that the costs would run 50 per cent more, or 1.5 per cent of covered pay roll.

For compulsory health insurance the low figure is based on Dr. I. S. Falk's estimate that after the system is fully established the costs will be about $50 per capita for 85 per cent of the population. That seems a safe figure to use as a low. For the high figures the estimate of approximately $100 per capita, proposed by Dr. Elizabeth W. Wilson, is used. As previously noted, she assumes that the introduction of compulsory health insurance would immediately lead to demands for coverage of the entire population and complete service. These demands, she believes, would promptly be met with resulting substantial increases in cost. Her assumptions of increased service and coverage, based on her extensive studies in the field and especially of British experience, appear sufficiently realistic to warrant using her figures for the upper range that can be anticipated. These figures would not, however, be reached without marked extension of current proposals.

For unemployment compensation the low estimate is based on 2 per cent of the pay roll used in estimating for H.R. 2893 and the high as 3 per cent of that pay roll.

The estimates for public assistance used here are somewhat higher than statements by government officials would suggest. They make allowance for the possibility that the open-end grant system with high percentages of federal participation will lead many states to liberalize their laws respecting eligibility and impose taxes earmarked for public assistance. Should this movement gain increased momentum, it will greatly increase public assistance payments before the insurance programs can be fully extended.

For veterans, estimates based on the material in Chapter VI are used.

According to these figures the low estimate for the four insurance programs would be 15.65 billion dollars in 1960 increasing to 26.25 billions at the end of the century. According to the high estimates the increase would be from 29.27 billion dollars in 1960 to 46.35 billions in the year 2000. If public assistance and veterans' benefits are added, the range would be from 21.55 to 32.75 billion dollars according to the low estimates and from 35.77 to 54.95 according to the high.

CHAPTER IX

METHODS OF FINANCING

In the earlier chapters dealing with specific government welfare programs, attention was directed to the costs of providing various benefits and services—with costs measured in terms of government expenditures. The preceding chapter summarized the benefits and costs. The purpose of this chapter is to present succinctly the balance of the information essential to an over-all appraisal of the whole program. Each welfare project will be considered separately to show the methods employed in raising the necessary money. Two of these, old-age and survivors insurance and unemployment compensation, involve the management of large reserve funds. Since there is considerable confusion with respect to the operation of government reserve funds, special consideration will be given to them. In the final section, the various methods of financing will be summarized. Emphasis will here be placed on the particular sources of funds used for the welfare project in its entirety.

OLD-AGE AND SURVIVORS INSURANCE

Under the existing system a tax of 1 per cent has been levied on the wage or salary up to $3,000 earned by individuals in covered occupations.[1] The employers in these lines of activity are taxed a like amount. The revenues are collected by the United States Treasury and under a permanent appropriation are credited daily to the OASI Insurance Trust Fund. Benefits and administration costs are charged to this Fund. The excess of revenues is then borrowed by the Treasury which places interest-bearing government securities in the Fund. The taxes were set at

[1] To be increased to 1½ per cent on January 1, 1950. Under the 1939 amendments the tax of 1 per cent on employees and employers was to have been in effect until the end of the calendar year 1942. It was to be raised progressively to 2 per cent at the end of 1942, to 2½ per cent at the end of 1946, and to 3 per cent at the end of 1948.

levels which would, in the first two to three decades, build up a large reserve of interest-bearing obligations.[2] In later years when the revenues would be inadequate to meet benefit payments, the deficiency would be made up in part by using the interest credited to the Fund.

Several changes are proposed in H.R. 2893. As shown in Chapter I, the coverage and benefits would be greatly increased. It has been estimated that costs would aggregate roughly 5 to 7 billion dollars in 1960 and 13.5 to 21 billions in the year 2000.[3] Beginning with 1950 these costs would be financed by a 2 per cent tax on both employee and employer,[4] by a tax of 2.25 per cent on the self-employed,[5] by a large draft on general tax revenues,[6] and by using the interest income of the Trust Fund. It is also proposed to raise the taxable wage and salary ceiling from $3,000 to $4,800. For ten years this level of taxes will provide a revenue surplus to be used to increase the Trust Fund.[7]

The operation of OASI has involved the establishment and building up of an Insurance Trust Fund. Under H.R. 2893 the Trust Fund will reach a maximum of roughly 30 billion dollars by 1960 [8] and will be held at that level indefinitely.[9] As noted above, this Fund reflects an excess

[2] This Fund now aggregates roughly 12 billion dollars.

[3] These figures are estimated on the basis of two sets of assumptions, thus giving a low-cost estimate and a high-cost estimate.

[4] There are certain exceptions. See H.R. 2893, sec. 301, (c), (d).

[5] The same, sec. 311.

[6] It is estimated that from 4.0 to 6.5 billion dollars of general revenues would be required to support the system by the end of this century. See Social Security Administration, Actuarial Study 28 (February 1949), p. 19.

[7] H.R. 6000, prepared by the Ways and Means Committee, has passed the House. This bill provides for a periodic stepping up of tax rates from 1½ per cent on employee and employer in 1950 to a maximum of 3¼ per cent on each in 1970. The tax rate on the self-employed is 50 per cent higher than that on the employee.

[8] Social Security Administration, Actuarial Study 28, pp. 19-20.

[9] Under H.R. 6000, the Fund will rise to 90 to 100 billion dollars around 1990 and will decline somewhat thereafter. See *Social Security Act Amendments 1949*, H. Rept. 1300, 81 Cong. 1 sess., p. 35.

of current revenues over current payments, with the surplus borrowed by the federal government. The result is the same as if the government were borrowing from the public or from the banking system—the lender receives interest-bearing obligations.

Experience with private insurance has revealed the necessity of establishing actuarial reserves to be invested in securities and mortgages that meet the requirements of regulatory laws. The income from these investments together with the receipts from insurance premiums [10] had to be adequate to meet the liabilities under the policies. In the event that the private company should cease writing new insurance and thereby eliminate any further premium receipts from new business, the gradual liquidation of the reserves plus investment income would be sufficient to pay all claims as they matured. In this manner, soundness and solvency of private insurance systems was achieved.

Until the 1930's the reserves of private voluntary insurance systems were, for the most part, invested in the bonds and preferred stocks of private industrial concerns, mortgages of farmers and home owners, and the bonds of local governments. That is, the funds were employed to promote directly or indirectly procreative enterprise. In the depression which started two decades ago, insurance companies invested an increasing proportion of their funds in federal government issues. This shift was occasioned not because of any inherent superiority of government bonds

[10] The laws required the life insurance companies to charge premiums which with the interest earned by the resulting reserves, would pay all claims. They were based on actuarial cost plus expense loading and were commonly although not necessarily "level." With a level premium the insured in his early years pays far more than the actual cost of his insurance protection in those early years so that he may pay far less than the actual cost of his protection in later years. His excess payments in the early years go into the reserve maintained with respect to his policy, and the interest earned by that reserve reduces the amount he has to pay as a level premium.

but because of the almost complete disappearance of new investment outlets in private enterprise.[11]

The establishment of the Trust Fund has given an aura of soundness and solvency to the OASI system. Many believe that this reserve fund "earns" income in the same sense as do private insurance reserves; that, if need be, all claims could be met by liquidation of the reserves; and that an individual, with his final payment of OASI taxes, will have paid in full for his retirement benefit.

The operation of the OASI Trust Fund is *not* similar in character to that of a private insurance company. Private insurance reserves, as noted above, are usually invested in projects that directly participate in or promote the production of goods and services. These investments are procreative in character and thus "earn" income. Furthermore, they are assets of the insurance company reserve, but they are liabilities of *other* enterprises. The OASI Trust Fund is invested in federal government securities. Since the money is used by the government in meeting its regular expenditure requirements, no real reserve is created. The obligations of the government (liabilities) deposited in a trust account do not represent assets; they merely record future obligations which can be fulfilled only through the levy of future taxes upon the economy in general. The Trust Fund is thus a fiction—serving only to confuse.

The explanation of the failure to establish trust fund assets analogous to those provided by private insurance companies is presumably that the sums ultimately involved are so stupendous that available investment securities of productive enterprises would not be adequate for the purpose. The deposit of its own liabilities in a so-called reserve fund thus appeared as a happy solution to the problem.

11 See Harold G. Moulton, George W. Edwards, James D. Magee, and Cleona Lewis, *Capital Expansion, Employment, and Economic Stability (1940)*, pp. 32-37, 93.

The total costs of the system, paid partly by special taxes and partly out of general tax revenues, would mount progressively over the next half century. The estimated total costs by decades under H.R. 2893 and the contribution of special and general taxes respectively is shown in the following table:

PAYING FOR OASI UNDER H. R. 2893 [a]

(In millions of dollars)

| Year | Total Costs [b] | Costs Paid by: | |
		Taxes on Employees, Employers, and Self-Employed	General Taxes [c]
1960	4,768	4,159	609
1970	7,698	5,979	1,719
1980	10,269	7,898	2,371
1990	12,390	8,388	4,002
2000	13,496	8,945	4,551

[a] These estimates relate to costs and financing under H. R. 2893 and were prepared in the Division of the Actuary, Social Security Administration. For purposes of illustration, we have used the "low-cost estimates financing Basis A." See Social Security Administration, Actuarial Study 28, p. 19.

[b] Includes costs of administration.

[c] Includes 536 million dollars interest on Fund.

The annual costs are estimated to rise from 4.8 billions in 1960 to 13.5 billions in the year 2000. It will be observed that in the early decades much the greater part of these costs will be paid by taxes on employers and employees. By the end of the century, however, about one third will have to be met out of general tax revenues.[12]

H.R. 6000 provides for lower costs and a different allocation of the burden of paying. The table on page 157 shows that annual costs will range from 3.8 billion dollars in 1960 to 11.7 billions in 2000. Under this plan the contributions

[12] The figures of the estimated cost borne by general taxes include 536 million dollars of interest on securities held in the Trust Fund. This interest is included because such payments to the Fund also have to be made out of general tax revenues. In early years, when special taxes exceed payments, interest due on the Fund will be paid with additional deposits of government bonds.

from general taxes begin much later, but by the year 2000 will constitute over 20 per cent of the total.

PAYING FOR OASI UNDER H. R. 6000 [a]

(In millions of dollars)

Year	Total Costs [b]	Costs Paid by:	
		Taxes on Employees, Employers, and Self-Employed	General Tax Revenues [c]
1960	3.8	5.9	—
1970	6.2	8.3	—
1980	8.4	8.6	—
1990	10.6	8.9	1.7
2000	11.7	9.2	2.5

[a] Estimates are from *Social Security Act Amendments of 1949,* H. Rept. 1300, 81 Cong. 1 sess., p. 35.

[b] Excludes administrative costs.

[c] Consists almost wholly of interest payments on the government bonds held by the Fund.

These estimates of the collections from special taxes on employers and employees assume general prosperity and a high level of employment. The general tax estimates are based on the same assumption. It is obvious that in the event of a business recession the collections would be sharply curtailed, while at the same time the volume of benefit payments would increase. Under such circumstances the government would presumably have to borrow the additional sums required.

The question whether the nation will have sufficient economic capacity to support this system will be considered in the following chapter. It may be pointed out, however, that so far as the taxes here imposed result in a higher level of prices the real protection given by the system will be proportionately decreased.

Before leaving the subject, it should be emphasized that this social security system as it would operate would provide substantial revenues for the general support of government for a considerable number of years—ten years under H.R. 2893, and as much as thirty years under H.R. 6000. Such revenues are sometimes called "forced contributions" from special groups for the benefit of the budget as a whole.[13] This result is inherent in a system based upon insurance concepts; for a time the collections will inevitably exceed the benefit payments.

The present plan tends to confuse the public as to the ultimate costs of the program and to obscure the true situation with respect to the federal budget. The direct costs of the system to those who participate are less in the earlier years than they will ultimately have to be; and the windfall source of revenues to the government in due course vanishes.

UNEMPLOYMENT COMPENSATION

The volume of unemployment, and hence the cost of compensation, will be determined at any time almost entirely by political and economic forces. Biological or natural factors are of almost no significance. Absence of any reliable method of forecasting economic conditions and the extent of unemployment means that a true insurance system to protect individuals against loss of jobs is impracticable. Unemployment compensation in the United States has not been developed by the application of mathematical or actuarial principles of insurance. The approach has necessarily been practicable, and in a sense, experimental rather than scientific. A decision was reached that a 3 per cent tax on covered pay roll could be paid by employers, and that the revenues would provide for a satisfactory unemployment compensation system.

[13] This excess payment may not properly be termed a "tax" since it is paid into the Trust Fund and not into the general tax revenues of the Treasury. Neither is it a loan by the employee, employer, and self-employed to the government. The borrowing-lending transaction takes place between the Fund and the Treasury and does not give rise to a contractual obligation to repay between the Trust Fund or the federal government and the worker. There exists only a moral obligation on the part of Congress to provide funds for pensions as people with an insured status reach retirement age.

The national law provides that all employers of 8 or more workers, excepting those in designated categories, shall be subject to an excise tax with respect to employment amounting to 3 per cent of that part of the pay roll that represents payments to individuals not in excess of $250 a month.[14]

Under the Social Security Act if a state adopted an unemployment compensation law which complied with the requirements of the federal act, an employer covered by both the federal and the state laws could deduct from the federal tax of 3 per cent the amount of the state tax up to 2.7 per cent. Naturally *all* states levied the full 2.7 per cent. Had they done otherwise, the difference between the 2.7 per cent tax and a lower tax would have to be paid by employers in the state to the federal government.

The federal act permitted the states, if they so desired, to establish systems of experience rating which might result in a reduction of the state tax actually paid by an employer below the 2.7 per cent. Under the federal act the employer who benefits by an experience rating deduction is given the same credit against the federal tax that he would have been allowed if he had paid the full state tax without the experience rating deduction. The amount of reduction (up to 2.7 points) depends upon the favorableness of the employment record of the employer. This "rating" device provides an incentive to management to adopt policies and practices designed to stabilize the level of employment and thus to reduce the volume of unemployment, for example, in seasonal slack periods or in times of change-over from an old model to a new one.

---

[14] There have been several proposals to change the method of financing unemployment compensation by taxing the employee as well as the employer. The Advisory Council on Social Security to the Senate Committee on Finance advocates a tax of three fourths of one per cent on each. Mr. Altmeyer, a prominent spokesman for the Administration, suggests a tax of 1 per cent on employee and employer and elimination of "experience rating." See *Recommendations for Social Security Legislation,* S. Doc. 208, 80 Cong. 2 sess., p. 140.

In order to establish a reserve fund, the original law prohibited any payments to the unemployed by the states for the first two years after the system started operations.[15] Owing to the high level of economic activity and employment over the past 10 years, revenues have been far greater than had been anticipated, and costs have been relatively small. In consequence, the reserve fund now aggregates more than 7 billion dollars, largely invested in government securities.

The fact that a reserve fund of such magnitude has accumulated in the first 13 years of the system has been regarded by some as evidence that benefits could be increased and taxes could be reduced, especially if the system were nationalized so that all would draw from a common pool. In fact, some studies have shown that, even in the event of fairly severe unemployment, covered workers could exhaust their benefit rights with a "balance" still remaining in the Fund—at a time when large-scale unemployment was continuing to be a national problem. It should be remembered, however, that use of the 7 billion dollar fund involves the redemption of these bonds out of tax revenues or by borrowing. In time of depression, this would mean an increase in the total borrowing requirements of the federal government. Were there no "balance" in the Fund, the government would surely provide funds to tide over the unemployed—funds that could be obtained only by borrowing.

The unemployment reserves do not belong to the national government or any of its agencies. They belong to the respective states and are held in trust for them by the United States. The law requires the states to pay all money received into the Fund. With minor exceptions these payments must be made immediately upon receipt of the taxes to the Secretary of the Treasury and are credited to the Unemployment Trust Fund.

[15] 49 Stat. 640.

The operation of the Trust Fund is similar to that of the OASI system. The Fund is not a segregated reserve of cash kept on tap for special emergencies. The soundness and solvency of unemployment compensation does not depend upon the existence of this Fund, but rests on the power of the government to tax. The building up of a large fund merely reflects the fact that, in addition to paying for current unemployment compensation, employers have contributed to the financing of general government activities by the amount in the Fund.

From the standpoint of finance another feature of the American system deserves comment. In periods of rising activity and employment, the effective tax rate and tax revenues will tend to decline under experience rating systems. Conversely, when business activity is receding the tax rate on the employer will increase. Whether revenues will increase will depend upon the volume of employment in conjunction with the effective tax rate. Thus tax rates will be relatively low in periods of prosperity and relatively high when there is much unemployment. The effect of the "rating" device is to increase the employers' costs and thus tend to restrain business expansion in the early stages of recovery.

MEDICAL CARE

The Administration has submitted a bill, H.R. 4312, which embodies a compulsory system of health insurance. All workers would be taxed 1½ per cent on their annual wages or salaries up to $4,800, and employers would be taxed a like amount. The self-employed would pay a tax of 2¼ per cent on their net income up to $4,800. General tax revenues would supply an amount not in excess of 1 per cent of covered pay roll.[16]

16 The bill itself does not specify any tax rates. The data were given in the testimony of J. Donald Kingsley, Acting Federal Security Administrator, *National Health Program, 1949,* Hearings before a subcommittee of the Senate Committee on Labor and Public Welfare, 81 Cong. 1 sess., p. 102.

The revenues resulting from these taxes would go, directly or indirectly, into a special fund from which would be paid the costs of personal medical care for those who had contributed enough to have acquired an insured status and their dependents. As in the case of an almost universal old-age and survivors insurance system, there would be some with no earnings or with such small earnings that they would not attain or maintain an insured status. They would have to be provided for in either of two ways: (1) They could, as at present, be given personal medical care without charge or without full charge, and the costs could be met from public or private funds, or charges could be withheld or not collected by the practitioners or the institutions. (2) Public funds could be used to pay the minimum amount required for an insured status on behalf of those without sufficient earnings to attain and maintain an insured status. General public funds could be used to retain an insured status for persons long unemployed and for all retired workers and their dependents, whether retirement was due to age or disability. The need for personal medical care is perhaps relatively greatest among those who have retired because of age or disability. Hence it must be assumed that any "no-means test" insurance system will make provision for them.

Some bills would afford medical care to the poor and the indigent through a federal grant-in-aid system. These grants would presumably be financed from general revenues without earmarked special taxes. The objective would be for the national government to co-operate with the states to assure satisfactory personal medical care to the poor and to the medically indigent. The federal government would establish in broad terms certain minimum requirements with which the state plan would have to conform if it were to be federally approved. Within these limits a state would be free to adopt any plan that seemed to meet its particular needs. It is assumed that the federal grant would be a lump sum from general revenues, the exact amount of which would be determined by an appropriate formula. Hence if an individual state should decide to adopt a compulsory health insurance plan, the federal grant would go into the fund to help meet the costs of medical care for those unable to contribute at full scale.

PUBLIC ASSISTANCE AND VETERANS' BENEFITS

Both of these programs are financed solely from general tax revenues. The over-all level of costs will be the significant factor effecting this method of financing. The demands on general revenues to pay for public assistance and benefits to veterans will in all likelihood show a continued and extensive growth. Veterans' benefits alone may mean annual appropriations of 7 to 10 billion dollars by 1990.

The analysis thus far has been focused on the progressive expansion of costs involved in the system and the respective contributions of special taxes levied upon employers and employees and the general taxes derived from the public as a whole. The following table shows the percentages of pay roll that would be taken from the employer and the percentages of earnings that would be taken from employee for the various types of benefits when the plan is fully matured some fifty years hence.

	Workers' Pay	Employers' Pay Roll	Self-employed Net Income
OASI [17]	2.00 per cent	2.00 per cent	2.25 per cent
Unemployment compensation	......	3.00	......
Medical care [18]	1.50	1.50	2.25
Public assistance	......	......	......

[17] H.R. 2893. The taxable ceiling is $4,800 of pay. Under H.R. 6000, the tax rates are 3¼ per cent on employee and employer, and 4⅞ per cent on the self-employed; drafts on general revenues would total about 2.5 billion dollars. The taxable ceiling is $3,600.

[18] H.R. 4312. The taxable ceiling is $4,800 of pay.

Employed workers would be taxed for OASI and medical care combined at the rate of 3.5 per cent. Employers would pay 6.5 per cent, including unemployment compensation. In the case of self-employed the contributions would equal 4.5 per cent of their net income. The multitude of individuals here involved would also have to contribute for these insurance features, together with veterans' benefits, their share of the 18 to 20 billions of general taxes used for the programs, including veterans' benefits.

It should be noted that these rates relate to gross earnings up to the level of $4,800, with no deductions akin to those allowed in income tax calculations. In short, this means that a married man with two children with a $4,000 income would contribute 3.5 per cent, or $140. The income tax of the same individual at present rates would amount to $200.

CHAPTER X
FISCAL COMPLICATIONS

The investigation thus far has been concerned chiefly with the social security program of the Administration. This program includes changes in old-age and survivors insurance and public assistance and the introduction of compulsory health insurance. The estimated future costs of this welfare plan have been summarized in Chapter VIII. Social security, however, is merely one of many governmental activities. It remains, therefore, to consider the over-all costs of government and the capacity of the nation to carry the load.

We shall be concerned with two questions: What is the present budgetary situation? Can the nation, in the decades to come, afford the vast expansion of welfare costs together with other governmental outlays?

THE BUDGETARY SITUATION

The present fiscal situation is precarious. The end of World War II has not been followed by a marked reduction in either governmental expenditures or taxes. Instead, the postwar years have been characterized by programs, both domestic and foreign, that call for continuing large-scale governmental expenditures and revenues.

Governmental expenditures. The expenditures of governments in the United States, national, state, and local, amounted to about 52 billion dollars in the fiscal year 1948—or nearly 25 per cent of the national income. Four items (all concerned with war and international affairs) accounted for about three fifths of this total. The figures are given below in millions of dollars:

National defense	$10,648
International affairs and finance	7,745
Veterans' services and benefits	6,563
Interest on the public debt	5,211
Total	$30,167

The domestic activities of government accounted for about two fifths of total expenditures. The three major domestic functions in terms of expenditures are education, public assistance, and highways. Agriculture and agricultural resources, other natural resources, and a broad group of general activities accounted for large expenditures of the federal government. At the local level, safety and public health are of major significance. These include police and fire protection, sewer and water systems, street cleaning and maintenance, and garbage disposal. Expenditures for public housing and hospitals will presumably mount in the future.

Many of these governmental programs involve long-time forward commitments. Benefits and other services to veterans, social security, and interest on the public debt all may be regarded as long-continuing obligations. Owing to political pressures education, public housing, and farm price support may occasion large outlays for a long period of years. The international situation is such that for years to come this country may well be under heavy expense for national defense and aid to friendly foreign countries for economic and defense rehabilitation. As shown in Chapter VI, outlays for veterans will increase as the veterans of World War II grow older. Interest on the public debt will depend on the rate of interest the government has to pay and the amount of debt outstanding. There is little likelihood that the public debt can be financed at significantly lower rates than at present. Nor, in view of the way fiscal matters are progressing at present, does a considerable reduction in the public debt appear promising.

While substantial reductions in aggregate expenditures might be achieved in the immediate future, there appears to be little resistance to the many political pressures opposing such cuts. In fact, there are growing and insistent demands for heavy additional expenditures for welfare, education, highways, health, and public safety.

The public school system is confronted with the problem of providing facilities for an unprecedented number of children, resulting from the increased birth rate. Many urban communities have had a large influx of population necessitating heavy outlays for school buildings and more teachers at higher salaries. Even communities with slower growth find it necessary to make up for school construction and maintenance deferred during the war and materially to increase teachers' salaries. State highway departments likewise deferred construction and maintenance during the war and are now confronted with higher costs for labor and material. Increased highway traffic, moreover, necessitates extensive and costly new roads, constructed to carry heavy loads safely at high speed, with suitable separation of grades at important intersections.

Governmental revenues. Tax revenues for all levels of government in the fiscal year 1948 amounted to roughly 51 billion dollars. This total excludes transfers to social security trust funds for benefit payments at the federal level and transfers of unemployment compensation taxes at the state level.

Taxes on income are the leading source of public revenues. In 1948 they supplied more than half (56 per cent) of the tax revenues for all levels of government. Individual income taxes provided 19.7 billion dollars and corporate income and excess profits taxes 10.4 billions. Of the 30.1 billions from these sources the national government received 29 billions or all but 1.1 billion.

Sales, use, and gross receipt taxes, either general or specific, ranked next to income taxes in yield. In 1948 they accounted for 11.7 billions or 21.7 per cent of the total tax receipts of all levels of government. Together with income taxes they accounted for more than three quarters (77.7 per cent) of all tax receipts in the United States.

Property taxes yielded only 5.5 billions or 10.8 per cent of the total. All but 282 millions of the property taxes were collected by local governments. These taxes supplied over 90 per cent of the tax revenues that local governments collected for themselves.

Social insurance taxes in 1948 amounted to 3.6 billions and accounted for 6.7 per cent of total tax receipts. Of the federal old-age and survivors insurance taxes one half or about 803 millions were levied against the pay of the covered workers and thus were in a sense income taxes; and the same is true of one half (280 millions) of the railroad retirement taxes. Thus about 1.1 billion might be added to the 19.7 billions collected through general personal income taxes. Most of the balance of the social security taxes (2.5 billions) are paid initially by employers on their pay rolls. Insofar as these taxes are shifted to consumers, they are disguised sales taxes.

In fiscal 1949—nearly an all-time peak in economic activity—there was a deficit of 1 billion dollars for all governmental activities. The outlook for 1950 is for a federal deficit of 5 to 6 billion dollars, according to official estimates; hence the President has suggested that it will be necessary to increase taxes.

THE FUTURE BURDEN

It should be noted that the enlarged old-age insurance system would, immediately speaking, ease the cash position of the government. This is because of the excess of revenues over disbursements in the early years—which under present procedure would be used to meet ordinary cash requirements of the government. Eventually, however, the situation would be reversed. For reasons already noted, a substantial portion of the social security costs will have to be met out of future general tax revenues. Thus the fiscal difficulties are deferred.

As shown in Chapter VIII, the cost of the social security program (excluding compulsory health insurance) and the veterans' program by 1970 would range from 19 to 25 billion dollars. What are the factors which will determine whether the United States can readily bear this load together with all other governmental costs? Whether the nation can carry it will depend on the one side on the growth of the national income and taxable capacity of the nation, and on the other side on the growth of federal expenditures in general.

Two factors will determine the growth of aggregate national income and hence taxable capacity: (1) the expansion of the labor force and (2) the increase in man-hour output. We leave out of consideration a possible rise in prices, because it produces no net gain.

The size of the labor force as far forward as 1970 can now be rather definitely forecast. The great majority of young people seek jobs between the ages of 15 and 25. Thus the bulk of the 30,000,000 children born in the 1940's would enter the labor force in the sixties. On the basis of past experience and allowing for those retiring from employment, the labor force by 1970 would aggregate approximately 75 millions. Assuming a high level of employment of, say, 95 per cent of the labor force, the national income would reach about 270 billion dollars as a result of this growth factor.

The second factor, increasing productivity, is of much greater potential importance. Studies of the volume of production as compared with hours worked indicate that over the four decades prior to World War II, the increase in productivity in manufacturing industry *averaged* as much as 3 per cent annually.[1] The increase varied widely in different industries and from time to time. In the first two decades the rate of increase averaged only 1.5 per cent annually, while in the last two decades it averaged 3.6 per cent. For the economy as a whole, including all types of economic enterprise, the increase in productivity

[1] Solomon Fabricant, *Employment in Manufacturing, 1899-1939* (1942), p. 331.

during this forty-year period was somewhere between 1.6 and 2.2 per cent annually.

There is no assurance, of course, that the experience of the past will be repeated in the future. In 1948 one authority commented on productivity for the period 1939-47 as follows: "Output per man-hour, during the past decade —that is, from about 1939—has not increased as rapidly as that 2 per cent average which we had learned to experience during many decades before World War II."[2] Estimates submitted by the Bureau of Labor Statistics, at a conference on productivity in 1948, supported this conclusion.[3]

If productivity in the economy as a whole should increase during the next two decades at the rate of 1 per cent a year, the national income—allowing for the larger labor force—would reach about 330 billion dollars; if the increase were at the rate of 2 per cent, it would rise to 400 billions—assuming in both cases a high level of business activity and employment.

On the basis of such projections of rising national income, some reach the comforting conclusion that the economy could readily carry the enlarged cost of the social security and veterans' benefits programs. With national income of the size indicated, tax revenues, assuming the continuation of the present level of rates, would run from 75 to 90 billion dollars—a figure well above the present level of governmental expenditures, plus the increased costs of the social security and the veterans' programs.

There can, however, be no assurance that such a rise in national income will occur. The situation in the world today is highly uncertain. Whether western Europe can achieve financial stability r e m a i n s an open question. Whether international economic recovery can be attained

[2] Solomon Fabricant, "Productivity Trends: Past, Present and Future." *Incentives, Payrolls and Social Costs* (1948), pp. 23-24.

[3] Jules Bachman, *Economics of a Fourth-Round Wage Increase* (1949), p. 42.

may well be doubted. The possibility of future war casts its ominous shadow over our lives and our prospects for future security.

On the domestic side we are also confronted with grave problems and uncertainties. Thanks to an exceptional combination of circumstances, we have had an extraordinary period of prosperity since the war; but even so we have not been able to lower materially the level of taxes nor have we achieved financial stability. We are subsidizing important sectors of the economy, and we are constantly expanding the scope of non-revenue-producing governmental enterprise. Meanwhile, we are hoping that an ever-rising level of business activity will enable the private sector, especially industry, to carry the expanding load of governmental overhead. One may well question whether the investment incentives are adequate, and one may fear that short-sighted labor policies may serve to check further increases in productivity.

There is as much reason to believe that governmental expenditures as a whole will increase in the future as that productivity and national income will continue to expand. The mere growth of population will of course entail a corresponding expansion in public outlays for a wide range of services. Pressures for an expansion of governmental outlays for the benefit of the American people will doubtless continue—especially in such fields as education, housing, sanitation, water supply, reclamation and irrigation, highways, and other public works.

For purposes of comparison with the projected growth in national income, it may be of interest to project forward to 1970 the growth of governmental expenditures; as in the case of productivity we shall project from 1950 to 1970 the rate of increase that occurred during the first half of the present century. In order to be conservative, we shall exclude in this period the rise in military expenditures and interest on the public debt.[4]

[4] Veterans' benefits are included in the projected costs for 1970.

Expenditures of government (excluding military outlays and interest on debt) rose from 1.1 billion dollars in
1902 to approximately 38.4 billions in 1949.[5] If governmental outlays continue to increase at this rate until 1970, they
would aggregate roughly 115 billion dollars—assuming no
change in prices. When account is taken of interest on the
public debt as of 1970 and the probable continuance of substantial military expenditures, the over-all costs of government would perhaps approach 140 billions. With such an
assumed rate of increase on the expenditure side, the financial position of the government would be completely under-
mined.

The actual future level of governmental expenditures
cannot of course be predicted with any definiteness. It
will depend upon a wide range of factors. On the one side
there will be continuing demands for more and better governmental services, while on the other side insistent demands for economy and for tax reductions may be expected.

In view of the uncertainty both as to the future taxable
capacity of the nation and the future financial requirements of government, a program which would commit for
decades to come a substantial proportion of governmental
receipts for the support of a particular social program—
irrespective of other needs or requirements—should be
subjected to most thorough consideration. This is especially the case since the present generation would be deciding for our children and grandchildren what proportion of their earnings should be devoted to these particular
services.

---

[5] This rise reflects both the expansion in governmental services and the
advance in prices, which amounted to 180 per cent.

CHAPTER XI

CONCLUSIONS

In this concluding chapter we shall set forth what we conceive to be the requirements for a financially sound social security system and how the funds necessary for such a system may best be raised. As a preliminary, it is necessary to summarize the basic shortcomings of existing and proposed systems. The truth is that the principles adopted and the methods employed in the setting up of the old-age part of the social security system have created a practical dilemma for the government. The issue here presented is so vital that a restatement of the nature of this dilemma is essential.

THE NATURE OF THE DILEMMA

The complications arise out of the attempt to apply private insurance concepts to a public system. The terms "insured status" and "legal or actuarial reserves" imply a resemblance to private voluntary insurance plans; but the resemblance is fictitious—for the reserves are not *real* reserves and the protection of the insured rests not on invested assets but solely on future taxable capacity.

The use of this insurance concept appeared to necessitate the assessment of special taxes against employers, employees, and the self-employed. Under such a contributory system the government can attempt to collect in each year through taxes on employers, employees, and other prospective beneficiaries the true actuarial cost of the future benefits which will have to be paid ultimately with respect to the services rendered in that year. In other words, it can attempt to operate, as do insurance companies selling ordinary life policies, on a level premium basis. Its premiums or taxes remain at a constant rate throughout the working life of a covered employee.

173

But as the old-age and survivors system started without any benefit load and will not take on its full benefit load for some fifty years, collection of actuarial level premiums as taxes necessarily produces for a time far more revenue than is needed to meet current benefit and administrative costs. A huge excess of receipts over expenditures is therefore created for the benefit of the actuarial reserve account. The government is then confronted with the problem—how to handle this money.

Private insurance systems simply invest the money in securities or other properties. But under the governmental system the volume of funds would ultimately be so large that ordinary investment outlets would be wholly inadequate. In view of this situation the alternative was for the government to borrow the excess insurance funds and evidence its indebtedness by placing government bonds in a so-called reserve.

The difficulty arises when the annual costs in due course come to exceed the receipts from the special taxes. At that time it will be patent that the United States governmental debt obligations held in the reserve fund are not earning assets. The government must then raise the necessary cash to meet benefit payments and other costs by general taxation or by borrowing in the bond market.

The taxpayers of today pay the special taxes uncomplainingly because they believe they are buying social security. They do not rebel against those taxes as they would against taxes levied for the general purposes of government. They do not appreciate that most of the proceeds of the pay-roll tax on wages up to $3,000, a regressive tax, are actually being used to finance current operations and that the assets of the fund are simply debt liabilities of the government. Many opponents of the reserve fund believe, moreover, that any large excess of social security taxes over immediate benefit payments encourages government extravagance or wastefulness.

Because of these objections, opponents of the level premium and the full reserve take the other horn of the dilemma. They advocate a so-called "pay-as-you-go system." The idea is to levy only such current social security taxes as are required to meet current benefit and administrative costs. As the benefit payments and administrative costs rise progressively, as they will for fifty years or more, the special taxes will rise. In their upward movement they will after some years equal and then exceed the level premium. The fact that they will ultimately substantially exceed the level premium does not disturb the advocates of this system. They point out that the children and the grandchildren will have to pay the costs of the benefits and administration in their day anyway, and it is immaterial whether they pay the sum in one social security tax or in a level premium social security tax plus the taxes necessary to pay interest and principal on the governmental debts held in the actuarial reserve. The only possible difference between the future taxes would be in their incidence, and no one can foresee conditions in the year 2000 with sufficient clarity to appraise the incidence of the taxes that will then be in use. This pay-as-you-go plan, it will be observed, discloses the hollow fiction of the idea that the system is genuinely contributory and that employers and employees through their taxes are providing real insurance for themselves.

Under this system, however, a time would come some fifty years hence when current taxpayers would be meeting the true costs of the system. But in the meantime persons who draw benefits will have paid or occasioned the payment of only a fraction of the true costs of their benefits. The present generation thus says, in effect, to future generations, "We do the promising, you do the paying."

The essence of this system may be stated as follows: We say that our generation will take care of such of our citizens as can prove *need* through means test public assistance, raising their resources to the requisite minimum. For those whose resources are above that minimum we do nothing unless they have been under the insurance system for the length of time prescribed by Congress for acquiring an insured status. We do not assume the load which we attempt to direct future generations to assume. We allege that we could not at present afford the cost of "no means" test payments to our old and disabled persons and those dependent on them. We assume that future generations can and will.

The way to avoid the dilemma of the current pattern of old-age and survivors insurance, with its pseudo resemblance to private insurance, is to abandon it entirely. In its place should be substituted a system that assumes responsibility for the full current load to the extent that provision seems socially desirable and can be made within our present capacity to pay. Then we can be on a genuine pay-as-you-go basis. Each year benefits will be paid to those in need of them and current taxpayers will supply the required funds. There will be no reserves, no level premiums, no taxes being increased according to a schedule contained in an act of Congress attempting to forecast the distant future and to bind children and grandchildren. Our generation would care for its own and trust future generations to do likewise.

FUNDAMENTALS OF A SOUND SYSTEM

The situation which the country now faces thus suggests the wisdom of adopting a social security system that provides suitably for old persons and others now in need, pays the costs from current revenues, and makes no long-term commitments with respect to future payments. Such a system would assure those who are at present in need or who may become in need in the near future that they will not suffer want. The legislation, however, would not attempt to tell the young and those of middle age what the government will do for them years hence if they fall victims of one of the major hazards. Many persons at the older ages have learned that savings which in their early and middle ages appeared ample now turn out to be inadequate. The difficulty is not that they do not get the amount of money promised, but rather that the money does not have the anticipated purchasing power. They have paid in more purchasing power than they get back.

In the early years of the present century many private and municipal retirement systems went on the rocks because they had promised old-age benefits which as the systems matured proved too costly to finance. Today persons are attaining positions of leadership who are too young to have been through the sobering experience of crumbling pension systems. The pensions the old people had been counting upon could not be paid in full if at all, although those who retired in the early years got them promptly, and the balances in the fund then appeared ample to the workers. The danger appears great that the mistakes of the past are to be repeated. The government might meet a severe cash stringency by promoting an upward spiraling of wages and prices, thus reducing the purchasing power of the dollar.

Upon the assumption that no person in the United States is to be permitted to remain in want, whatever the cause of that want, the country has its choice among several types of systems which differ widely in the amount of taxation they require. Four will be here briefly outlined, arranged in the ascending order according to their costs and the taxes they would require. It will be understood of course that there are almost countless intermediate variations, but these four represent successive steps upward in governmental control over the way persons spend their earnings.

All four types are applicable in making provision for old age and total and permanent disability and for survivors and dependents unable to support themselves. The basic principles of the first three are also applicable to compensation in the event of unemployment and temporary disability that suspends or drastically reduces current earnings. Under either of the first two, distinctions between public assistance and insurance could be eliminated by financing the system through universal, flat-rate income taxes which make all workers contributors. These four types have no direct bearing on compulsory health insurance, which will require separate consideration. The four steps are:

1. Assurance of a standard minimum amount of purchasing power. Under such a system the government determines how much an individual, or each member of a family of a given age, sex, or condition must have to be able to live in accordance with the minimum standard established. If it is determined that for any reason the individual or the family lacks the specified amount, the government makes up the difference. This system involves minimum expenditures of public funds and the lowest taxes and leaves the people maximum freedom in the use of their income.

2. Payment of a standard minimum amount to all eligibles of a given class without reference to their other available resources. Under this system, upon the occurrence of a covered contingency, the individual or the family receives the exact and full sum fixed by the legislature for such time as the eligibility continues. Distinctions are made with respect to sex, age, number in family, and so on. The amount allowed is kept at a conservative minimum health and decency level to preserve in a large measure the freedom of the individual to use his earnings and resources as he sees fit. The smallness of the allowance, in theory at least, encourages the individual to make further provisions voluntarily.

3. Payment of something approaching a standard minimum amount to all eligibles but with additional amounts to those who have had higher earnings up to a relatively low maximum. The benefits would not advance proportionately with earnings. Since wages and earnings are to some extent related to levels and costs of living, this system establishes some relation between benefits and customary living levels or costs. It still adheres to the principle, however, that social security systems should do no more than put a low floor of protection under the workers and leave them a high degree of freedom in the use of their resources. It would not give increased benefits for increased length of covered service, a factor which substantially increases costs and the amount of taxes required.

4. Payment of benefits related to earnings up to a level so high that for a substantial part of the workers all their earnings would fall within the system. The philosophy here is to insure on the basis of customary purchasing power and not on that of minimum requirements of health and decency. It might be called a universal retirement system rather than a device exclusively to insure against want. Operated on a contributory basis, with the taxes paid by the workers a percentage of covered wages, it would probably be highly unacceptable to the public without increased benefits for increased length of service. This provision is costly. The taxes might become so high that many workers would have little or no margin for personal voluntary savings. The promised benefits might appear to be so nearly adequate that for many persons incentives for such savings would be destroyed. Thousands will become as children, looking to the maternal state to direct and provide. To make the system operate successfully, the state would have to compel compliance with its dictates.

All four systems necessitate taking from those with the larger earnings to provide for those who cannot provide for themselves. The extent to which this redistribution is involved would be least where need alone is met, and it would increase as the level of benefits and amount of compensation counted are increased. Political forces would determine the degree to which redistribution would be effected.

Our recommendation would be that benefits should not exceed the amount required to provide a minimum health and decency standard and that if persons desire more than that they should strive to obtain it through voluntary methods. To us the payment of benefits only to those who do not have the necessaries and only to the extent they lack them seems to preserve to maximum extent personal freedom and initiative. If government reports and investigations to determine resources are deemed too objectionable to be politically acceptable, then a flat uniform benefit would be the safest system in the present uncertain world.

A system that provides a minimum health and decency benefit only, whether the benefit is paid to all regardless of resources or only to those in need to the extent of their need, would not require the elaborate and costly paraphernalia of insurance. The question whether a citizen of the United States is or is not to receive a substantial allowance from funds raised by taxation should not turn on whether he has ever paid or even had opportunity to pay in the form of an earmarked special tax a fraction of the cost of that allowance. Legislative decisions on this point are inevitably arbitrary and sometimes, for administrative reasons, highly discriminatory.

The system that guarantees a standard minimum amount of purchasing power, it should be noted, would permit a fairly simple solution of the problems presented by veterans' benefits and annuities or other grants from public or private retirement systems. If the individual is already receiving the amount of purchasing power established as a reasonable minimum amount, he would not be eligible to receive further sums from social security taxes. If it be desired to give special recognition to veterans and their dependents, the objective could readily be accomplished by providing either (a) that veterans' benefits not in excess of a specified amount shall not be counted as an available resource in determining eligibility or (b) that the minimum amount of available resources established as a standard of eligibility shall be higher for veterans and their dependents than for nonveterans. Veterans in the next thirty years will have to pay a substantial part of the costs of both veterans' benefits and social security benefits. If both systems are high cost, the veterans will have to pay the resulting high taxes.

Either the guarantee of a minimum of purchasing power or the payment of a standard minimum amount to all eligibles of a given class without reference to their other available resources would not impede the development of public or private retirement and welfare systems worked out by employers and employees through bargaining or related processes. Under the less costly system of minimum purchasing power the retirement benefits of private systems would be the first line of defense; the beneficiary would come in on the general fund only if the private system did not provide him with the established minimum. A flat benefit paid to all regardless of their means would naturally and easily be taken into account in establishing or modifying public or private systems. They would be designed to provide benefits in addition to the minimum under the uniform governmental system.

FINANCING THE SYSTEM

A fundamental and apparently inescapable fact is that at any given time the active workers engaged in production must supply the great bulk of the goods and services consumed by those drawing social security benefits. Only to a limited degree would past production supply current needs, although the capital equipment obtained through past savings might be an important factor in determining the output of current workers. Thus each generation of productive workers would have to take care of those not currently productive, to the extent that the law would require.

Conditions at the time benefits are paid will largely determine how the costs of those benefits are actually distributed. If there are wide variations in income or earnings between the rich and the poor, government can get the required cash by progressive taxation. On the other hand, if the variations were reduced to a narrow range, the costs would have to be widely distributed. In the twenties a forecaster could have predicted with a feeling of assurance that a substantial part of the burden of social security benefits could be placed on the rich and the well to do. In 1949 the evidence indicates that not much more of the burdens of government could at present be assessed against the rich and the well to do and that as the burdens are increased in the near future they will bear more heavily on the great body of workers of moderate means. What the situation may be in subsequent years is unpredictable.

Today strong pressures are being exerted in an effort to place a substantial part of the costs of social security benefits on employers through the use of pay-roll taxes. These taxes become part of the labor costs and hence part of the costs of production of goods and services. It is extremely doubtful whether any substantial part of such taxes actually "stick" to employers, for in the long run if employers are to stay in business, they must recover their costs of production, and especially their out of pocket labor costs, including the pay-roll tax. The pay-roll tax on employment gives a competitive advantage to employers who make large use of labor-saving devices, and as between competing industries such as coal, oil, and natural gas to the one in which labor is the least important factor. The conclusion seems inescapable that the tax on the employer's pay roll has no necessary relationship to his real capacity to pay. The appearance of making the employer pay does, however, give real satisfaction to many workers, and hence it has great political advantages.

The use of pay-roll taxes paid by the employer gives rise to the question: What benefits should be given to and what taxes levied against the self-employed, particularly farmers? The position is often taken that since they have no employer to share in the cost they should either get less or pay more personally. Two points are important here. First, part of the taxes on employers may be passed along to the self-employed. Second, pay-roll taxes levied against an employer do not necessarily go to pay the benefit costs for his own employees. In the case of employers with mainly upper-bracket workers, the employers' taxes will as the system matures pay the benefits for low-paid workers of other employers. Thus the low-paid employee can share in the proceeds of the tax on employers, whereas the farmer or other independent worker of small means cannot to the same degree unless his benefits are the same and his personal payments the same.

Taxes on net income paid by the recipient have certain marked advantages as a source of funds to pay benefit costs. They are related to capacity to pay, even if assessed at a uniform, flat percentage rate. They do not become an element in the cost of production and hence cannot to any marked extent be passed along to consumers. Their use as earmarked taxes for social security would make the payer acutely aware of the immediate costs of the program and of the mushrooming costs. If applied without exemptions, they will give to every person with income the right to feel that he has paid for his social security at the same rate on his income as others have paid. Its use would facilitate doing away with the present arbitrarily determined insured status and would justify immediately assuming the load for all who are in need according to the legal definition of need.

The uniform flat rate income tax without exemptions coupled with the immediate assumption of full load might prove to be intensely unpopular because of costs. It would tend, however, to lessen the belief that someone else will pay the costs. The significance of factors such as the size of benefits, maximum benefits, and increasing benefits with length of service, would be brought home to everyone. The pressures on Congress would be better balanced than they are at present.

The tax of a given flat sum alike for all in a specified class regardless of their income cannot be used as the exclusive device for financing social security programs. The maximum amount which can be charged persons of low income is insufficient to pay the costs of their benefits, even if the benefits are uniform and modest. Under such a system the well to do pay the same sum as the poor, and what they thus contribute will not meet the costs of their own benefits. The flat sum alike for all would have to be supplemented from general revenues.

The use of the flat sum and the uniform benefit alike for all creates an attractive appearance of equal treatment of all citizens and a resemblance to voluntary insurance in which payment of like premiums buys like protection for all in a class. The resemblances, however, are fictitious because a substantial part of the costs are met and have to be met in other ways. The flat sum system likewise tends to encourage the use of the concept of the insured status which leaves the poorest to be cared for through public assistance. Use of the flat sum and the insured status necessitate, moreover, elaborate records and accounts, although they are far less complicated than those where benefits are related to past earnings and tax payments.

Sales taxes are a possible device for financing social insurance programs. A popular proposal is that a transaction tax at a given rate be levied and all the proceeds distributed monthly among persons declared eligible by

law with the proviso that each recipient must spend his
allowance practically immediately. Such a system would
probably result promptly in that upward spiraling of prices
and wages that is the dangerous disease to which social
security systems are peculiarly subject. The Congress
would of course use a sales tax to supply the sums needed
for social security benefits, varying the rate from year to
year so that the fund or account would always be in approximate balance. The sales tax is practically universal in its
application and would give to everyone the feeling that
he had paid and that he is continuing to pay even when
on benefit. It is, however, a regressive tax. Too much
weight should not be attached to that argument when progressive taxation which bears very heavily on the rich and
well to do is already in use for many other purposes of
government. The sales tax would presumably be even
more unpopular than the income tax and serve as a brake
on demands for increased liberality which results when
costs are hidden.

Immediate assumption of full load, payment of benefits
no greater than are necessary to give full protection against
need, and financing through a universal flat-rate personal
income tax earmarked for social security appears to be the
best system for use in the present uncertain times. Brought
face to face with full load costs to be met annually, the
people will be in a better position than they are now to
determine whether individuals with personal income sufficient to protect them from need should be paid a benefit
equaling that given to individuals who without the benefit
would be in need. Decisions on such vital matters should
be arrived at with full knowledge of the size of the true
load and the real costs of the system.

The American people and the Congress have at present
an opportunity to reconsider the fundamentals of the social
insurance systems that may not come again. Because of

the upward spiraling of wages and prices that has occurred since 1939, the money benefits now being paid under the most costly part of the program—old-age and survivors insurance—are comparatively small. They are small enough so that at present the existing system could without great difficulty be converted into one designed primarily to insure against the dangers of want, whatever the cause of that want, and that will to a high degree preserve the freedom of the individual to determine what use he will make of his earnings. Such a system will leave a wide field open for the voluntary savings that have been the source of capital, particularly venture capital.

COMPULSORY HEALTH INSURANCE [1]

The cost of compulsory health insurance would probably depend in large measure upon the methods used for compensating the practitioners, and the number of additional government employees required for its administration.

To minimize the revolutionary character of the proposals, it is commonly provided that the fee-for-service basis of compensating practitioners shall be one of the devices. The per-capita method and especially the salary method are played down to lessen the effectiveness of the charge of socialized medicine. The insurance method of payment would encourage many of the insured greatly to increase their demands for medical care. The fee-for-service method of paying the practitioners offers them a financial incentive to encourage this demand. There is no reason to believe that the experience in the United States would be different from that in other countries. The fee-for-service system would greatly increase costs.

Increasing costs and increasing taxes would result in demands for substitution of the other two methods, per capita or salary, that would presumably be much cheaper although more socialistic. The danger of these two cheaper

[1] The question of the wisdom of adopting compulsory health insurance is not considered in the present book.

methods is that they might seriously impair the quality of medical care which, however, is not a cost factor in the narrow sense of the word.

Whatever the method of compensation used, compulsory health insurance might lead to increased costs through the unnecessary use of expensive methods of treatment. Neither the practitioner nor the patient would be under compulsion to consider costs. To protect the system from excessive costs, the government would have to adopt regulations governing the practitioners in their employment of expensive methods. Advance approval by governmental representatives might be required before the practitioners could go ahead, and if the patient should desire a treatment or a procedure more expensive than the government approves, he would have to pay for it from his own resources. Under a governmental system everyone in theory would be entitled to the same treatment, and the government would have to establish the level that would be a proper charge against the insurance fund.

INDEX

INDEX